Broken
Signposts

Broken Signposts

HOW CHRISTIANITY MAKES SENSE OF THE WORLD

N. T.
WRIGHT

HarperOne
An Imprint of HarperCollins*Publishers*

HarperOne

FIRST EDITION

Designed by SBI Book Arts, LLC

Library of Congress Cataloging-in-Publication Data is available upon request.

ISBN 978-0-06-256409-2

20 21 22 23 24   LSC   10 9 8 7 6 5 4 3 2 1

Contents

Preface

SOME YEARS AGO I WROTE A PRIMER ON THE CHRISTIAN faith called *Simply Christian* (HarperOne, SPCK, 2005), in which I used four great themes—justice, spirituality, relationships, and beauty—as the starting point. These four themes had crystallized in my mind, slowly and over some years, as I tried to think through the Christian message in relation to wider issues in human life and society.

I was at the time working in various jobs that required me to live at the tricky intersection of church and state as well as with the perennial pastor's and preacher's challenge of relating the real gospel to the real world. In that book I described these four as "echoes of a voice": when we ponder them, it's as though we are hearing someone calling to us from just around the corner, out of sight. I suggested that, though these four do not themselves necessarily point to the truth of God or of Christian faith (many people appreciate their importance without finding themselves drawn into worshipping the God revealed in Jesus), when we think through the Christian story and its meaning with these questions in mind, there is a natural "fit" that is more than rough coincidence.

I have reflected on these four themes a good deal since then, and as my thinking has developed, I have added three more items that we also experience as echoes of this voice: freedom, truth, and power. It now seems to me, though this would need to be argued more fully, that we need all seven to be "in play" if we want to work toward a wise, mature human life and society. And I have come to see these seven not simply as "themes" or "questions," but as *signposts*. *Signposts* name a reality and point us in a direction. Likewise, these seven signposts name realities that all human cultures value as well as pointing beyond themselves to the meaning of life, to the meaning of the world. They indicate, in fact, how we ought to "make sense" of the world—how we ought to understand the way the world is and the challenge of being human within it. The fact that we care about them and are puzzled by them is itself telling us something about the deep "sense" of the world.

But by themselves they may not tell us all we would like to know. That is why, in another more recent book, *History and Eschatology: Jesus and the Promise of Natural Theology* (Baylor University Press and SPCK, 2019), I describe them as "broken signposts." The point there is that the seven themes do indeed appear to function as signposts that would enable us to make sense of the world—their constant appearance in different guises in everything from grand opera to newspaper editorials makes that clear enough—but that they all let us down. That "brokenness," however, turns out to be crucial in discerning what they really mean.

For that to make sense, though, we need to bring a different voice into the conversation. In my earlier treatment I discussed the seven "broken signposts" in relation to the Christian message in general. Here I want to do something quite different and invite the Gospel According to John to come on stage and address us on the topic. No doubt there are other parts of the Bible we could call on in the same way, but I have a hunch, which this book will explore, that John will provide fresh and often unexpected insight and show us the ways in which the seven themes really do function as signposts, albeit broken ones, while finally enabling us to make sense of the larger world within which they are such vital but difficult issues.

I am, as in many times past, grateful for the encouragement and editorial help I have received from Mickey Maudlin at HarperOne, and on this occasion also from Jana Reiss.

This book is dedicated to my old friend and colleague Carey C. Newman. For nearly thirty years now our paths have intertwined at both scholarly and personal levels. His friendship, encouragement, and taste in highland irrigation have been a consolation in difficult times and a delight in good ones. He would probably have wanted to edit the present book somewhat differently, but as in some other areas I presume we will continue to enjoy our disagreements as much as our many, and deep, agreements.

TOM WRIGHT
Wycliffe Hall, Oxford
Epiphany 2020

The Seven Signposts

T HE FRENCH PHILOSOPHER JEAN-PAUL SARTRE ONCE suggested a definition of hell as "other people." As an extrovert, I couldn't possibly agree with that statement, but in any case I have my own alternative candidate. For me, hell is the incomprehensible instructions that come with flat-pack furniture. I get down awkwardly on the floor, trying not to kneel on the smaller elements of the puzzle I have done my best to spread out in a sensible pattern. I read the instructions again. Perhaps the manufacturers put in the wrong ones?

Nothing seems to fit. Yes, here are the two sections of the wardrobe that correspond to the those in the picture on the box—we had to buy flat-pack because our old wardrobe wouldn't go through the new bedroom door—but where is the joining bit? How on earth do these little metal gizmos work, and how can I possibly do what the instructions say, screw them in place, without growing a third hand to hold it all together while tightening it? How can I make sense of it all?

The really annoying thing is that it looks as though it ought to work. I've done it often enough to know the sequence of emotions. I begin with such high hopes: the picture on the box tells me that this is exactly what we need against that bedroom wall. All we have to do is to put it together! But after half an hour of struggle I feel my confidence ebbing away. Robert M. Pirsig, in his 1970s classic *Zen and the Art of Motorcycle Maintenance*, describes a moment like this when his hero tries, and fails, to fix something on the motorcycle. He calls it the "hiss of escaping gumption." That is spot-on. *We know it ought to make sense, but we can't make it do so.* And the moment we admit that, morale drops dramatically. We can't understand why something that ought to fit together seems not to, and why we ourselves can't fix it, can't put it right, can't get the wardrobe together, can't (in that sense) "make sense" of it, literally making whatever it is into the "sense" that it ought to have. There may come a point when we want to throw the whole kit out the window.

Which brings us back to Jean-Paul Sartre, and to the point of this book. Human beings regularly experience the world as a whole as something that ought to make sense. There are several signs, clues if you like, of the sort of sense it ought to make. But things don't work out the way they seem to suggest.

Take two obvious examples, which we shall explore further in due course. We all know that justice matters, but even in the best systems mistakes are made, innocent people are convicted, criminals get away with it, and we start to distrust judges, juries, and the whole system. Similarly, we all know that relationships matter, but we all manage, with depressing frequency, to misunderstand one another, to hurt each other, to damage even our most important relationships, sometimes forever. That is the point where Sartre suggested throwing the whole kit out the window: life, he said, is just a sick joke.

The world promises so much, smiling alluringly, telling us how good things are going to be, but it never turns out like that, and even if it does for a while, there is a dark, mean truth to be faced soon enough that underlines Sartre's skepticism. Some bold philosophers have suggested that, even if death means total annihilation, we can still make sense of the world. But for many people that seems like whistling in the dark.

So what do we say about the signposts, the features of our world that, like the picture on the flat-pack box, seem to indicate that we can and should "make sense" of it—in both meanings: that we should be able not only to understand what life is all about ("making sense of it" as in "understanding why things are as they are"), but also to contribute creatively to it ("making sense of it" as in working toward fresh, creative ways forward)?

In this book I approach this question along two quite different, but converging, pathways. On the one hand, I explore what I call seven "broken signposts," the features of our world that, like the two I just mentioned, justice and relationships, appear to point to some real and lasting meaning, but that all too often let us down at the crucial moment. These seven signposts are recognized as such, I think, by more or less all societies at all times in history. Across very different cultures, human beings have known that these things are important and equally have wrestled with the fact that they usually couldn't quite make sense of them.

The great philosophers have written about these things in the abstract. Plato's *Republic*, for example, addresses the question of justice, and his *Symposium* is a discussion of love. The great novelists and dramatists have done so too; and a host of lesser lights have filled in the details, so that even the most tawdry television sitcom still focuses on fairness, friendships, freedom, and the rest. This points to the fact that these things are central to our world, vital in our lives, and still deeply puzzling. That, then, is the first pathway: to look more closely at these seven signposts and to explore what their brokenness might tell us.

The second pathway, on the other hand, offers a fresh way in by examining in some detail a text that the followers of Jesus of Nazareth have seen from very early on as central and life-giving. My main argument in this book is that when we understand the Christian message, we will see that it does indeed "make sense" of our world, because it helps us both to understand the world the way it is and to be able to contribute fresh "sense" through our own lives. But it would be a large task to try to set out the entire Christian message as a whole, and I have chosen here to focus on one text—the Gospel According to John—which I believe offers sharp and often surprising insights into these questions, which all humans in all societies have seen as vital.

The Gospel According to John, the fourth gospel in the Christian New Testament, has been much loved for nearly two thousand years. People of great wisdom and spiritual insight have found it a never-ending source of inspiration. Learned thinkers have pondered it. Millions of sermons have been preached on it. Its opening line—"In the beginning was the Word"—rings out over the airwaves every December from a thousand Christmas Eve services. It is a sentence we instantly perceive as simple in itself but endlessly profound in its many possible implications.

Some of John's great set-piece scenes—the learned Nicodemus coming to Jesus by night, the raising of Lazarus from the dead, "doubting Thomas" reaching out his hand to touch Jesus's wounds—have been painted by great artists and set to wonderful music by gifted composers, and so are etched into the world's imagination. Yet this gospel, endlessly profound, a thing of beauty in its own right, is not usually where people go when they want to reflect on the seven signposts. I think it's time we did just that.

In putting together the challenge to "make sense of the world" and the invitation to take a fresh look at John's gospel, I am taking a deliberately different stance from those who would see the whole point of the message of Jesus as providing an escape from the world. In many varieties of Christian faith and life people have by implication agreed, at least in part, with Sartre: life is unpleasant and meaningless and the best thing to do is to swap it for a better world, usually referred to as "heaven." I well understand how, in a world where brutality and corruption often appear to be the norm and where sickness or "natural disasters" threaten whole communities, one might come to that conclusion—and how people facing such appalling threats might look at me, a comfortable Westerner, and think, "You don't know how tough it really is." I take the point.

But part of the Christian faith from the start has always been the conviction that the God revealed in and through Jesus is precisely the creator of the world and that he has promised to put it right. That is the basis on which, even at the darkest times (which can strike us comfortable Westerners too in various ways), the answer is not to escape the world but, insofar as we can, to "make sense of it" in both of the ways I have indicated. That is the point of this book.

So what are these seven signposts, and how shall we tackle

them? I have already mentioned two obvious ones, justice (fairness, a sense that things need to be "put right") and relationships (focusing on that much-abused word "love," but radiating out in all directions). As I mentioned, in a previous book (*Simply Christian*) I added two more: spirituality and beauty. I now want to add three more—freedom, truth, and power—making seven in all.

These words don't tell you very much. They are inadequate labels. In fact, the closer we get to the reality the words evoke, to the real questions they pose to us, the more inadequate they seem. They give away as much as a passport photograph does of the person you love best. But they will work for the moment. Each of the seven names one of the big questions of life. Together they serve as foundations for more or less every other aspect of how we as humans relate to one another and the world.

My point is that in each case we face the same puzzle. All seven are widely seen as ways of "making sense of the world." The ancient Romans believed that their justice system would make sense of it all. Machiavelli argued—and many have put his ideas into practice—that naked power is what's needed, even if you have to lie and cheat to make it work. America celebrates its long tradition of freedom. And so on. It's as though we all know that these things will help us make sense of our world, but most of us aren't sure how to put the whole thing together (again, like my flat-pack furniture).

We can try to avoid these signposts if we choose, but they will reappear. Sometimes they seem to sneak up on us from behind just when we thought we were rid of them. They constitute the puzzles that lie behind most of the news stories. They are underneath the challenges that politicians would love to resolve once and for all, but never can. They nag away at us in the pages of a great novel. They nudge our elbow as we ponder a poem. Most of them come up, one way or another, in every good movie. The stresses and strains of family life bring them to our attention once more. They are fascinating, yet frustrating. Reflecting on them is every philosopher's pastime. Leaving them unresolved is every philosopher's nightmare. They really do appear to hold the key to making sense of our world, to understanding what it means to be human, to what it means for us human beings to flourish and thrive.

Every philosophy, every religion, every political system, every society holds by implication some kind of view of the seven signposts I have in mind. In fact, every single child, woman, and man has a view about them as well, though many people just take them for granted—until something goes wrong and then suddenly the relevant signpost comes back again in the form of a challenge, a question, or a puzzle. If you try to ignore any of them, they can and will take their revenge. A genuinely human life—a genuinely *wise* human life—is one that learns to recognize these signposts, puzzling though they often are, and to wrestle with their meaning intelligently and with sensitivity to the many other people who are trying to do the same thing in their own way. Perhaps these seven function something like those security systems in which you can only get into the innermost safe if all seven independent key holders show up and work together.

However, the signposts are themselves not only puzzling, but, as I shall explain, "broken." We once had a family holiday in a remote rural area where we were trying to find our way around along back country roads—only to discover that, whether by accident or intentional trick, some of the signposts at various crossroads had been turned so as to lead us off in quite the wrong direction. That's what it's like with all seven of the "signposts" I have listed. Some of them, indeed, seem actually to be pointing in the opposite direction: if we stress relationships, we may well create a world in which some people feel that their freedom is compromised—and vice versa. That dilemma lies behind many tense family situations and many dangerous political problems. Again, many have accused Christians (and other people of faith) of so concentrating on spirituality that they have forgotten about justice; and, again, believers have often turned the accusation around, especially against atheistic rulers. As for truth and power, we often talk of the need to "speak the truth to power," and one of the things that powerful people have all too often done is to suppress the truth.

The question then arises: Are these seven just illusions? Are they vestigial memories of the various things our distant ancestors had to navigate in their need to feed, to mate, to fight, or to flee? If so, does that mean that there's nothing more to them— that the whole thing, once again, is just a sick joke? If so, then the only thing to do might be to get what you can out of life and let the devil take the hindmost.

Wait a minute. Where did the devil come in? "Oh, it's just a manner of speaking," people will say. Well, perhaps. Or perhaps not. Does the fact that we all are aware of these seven, that we try somehow to live by them, but that we all still seem to get it wrong, mean that there is after all a fatal flaw in the world, a twist in the cosmic tale, something actively stopping us getting at the underlying reality or meaning of life? Might it be the case that we will never "make sense" of the whole thing? Some have thought so, though this problem, like the puzzling signposts themselves, remains a mystery.

In any case, it doesn't take much familiarity with real life, or with the classic plays, operas, novels, and poems of every culture, to see that these seven are indeed themes of universal importance. We are all trying to make sense of our world, and even if these signposts are "broken"—in the sense that each of them leads us forward and then leaves us frustrated—we know they matter vitally.

If these signposts appear to provide us, in however oblique a way, with clues as to how we might make sense of our world, do they also provide us with pointers to the possibility of a Creator, a God who made the world and still cares for it? Many have thought so, suggesting that our innate sense of justice, freedom, and the other qualities points to the strong possibility that we humans are made to reflect, in our very instincts, something of the character of this Creator. But this view has been under such sustained attack in the last two centuries that we cannot simply assume it; and, indeed, the "brokenness" of the signposts has been seen, again and again, as meaning that no such inference can be made.

I argue in *History and Eschatology* that once we grasp the fuller picture that has Jesus of Nazareth at its center, these signposts can indeed be retrieved: they were after all pointing in the right direction, even though in their "brokenness" they were unable to give us the full instructions we would have needed. My approach here is different. By looking closely at one of the most important early Christian retellings of the story of Jesus, I want to suggest that we can indeed use these signposts to make sense of our world, in that we can both gain fresh understanding of the way the world is and make a real contribution to the fresh "sense" that the Creator wills for his creation.

Chapter One

Justice

WE WERE HAVING DINNER WITH FRIENDS. THE HUS-band is an academic colleague of mine, but since he lives on the other side of the world, we don't meet that often. He and I were looking forward to chatting about many things—who was researching what, the latest theory on St. Paul, who should be the next professor at such-and-such a university, and so on. But the seating plan for the meal didn't work out that way. Instead, my friend was seated next to my wife, whose interest in academic biblical studies ranks slightly lower than my interest in the biology of the earthworm.

He and she didn't know one another that well. But almost at once he asked her what she was reading. And, from the other end of the table, I saw her face light up. She mentioned one crime writer, then another. Yes, he was reading them too! And within seconds they were exchanging comments, comparing favorites, and finally swapping email addresses.

What is it about crime novels? Some people have teased me that *of course* my wife likes crime novels because, being married to a bishop, she has had too close-up a view of the twisted side of life. Well, maybe. But I think there is more.

The thing about crime novels—and this isn't rocket science, but it helps me understand what's going on—is that *justice is done in the end*. The mystery is solved. The murderer is identified and, normally in the genre, apprehended, charged, and convicted. There is a collective sigh of relief. I don't myself care for the grisly or gory bits in stories like that, but I can well understand the satisfaction of seeing everything put right at last.

It is a universal human longing. We all know that things are out of kilter: in the world, in my country, in your country, in my neighborhood and yours, in my family and perhaps in yours. If we were given a blank sheet of paper and asked to write down the names of people who had done something wrong to us, most of us wouldn't have much difficulty filling the page. If we were honest, we might also be able to compile a list of people to whom *we* had done something wrong. And most of those wrongs go unaddressed. Like untreated wounds, they fester.

That is how wars start: long-term grievances, something not put right. The history of the twentieth century, in Europe in particular, is the story of how perceived injustices gnawed away at this or that nation or people until finally "something needed to be done." Tragically, the "something" that was then done produced more grievances, more cascading effects. The "law of unintended consequences" kicked in, and the world is still wondering which of those "consequences" need now to be "put right" and which ones can be glossed over. When we look at the Middle East today, we only have to think of certain countries—Lebanon, Syria, Iraq, Egypt, not to mention Israel and Palestine—to call up a list of perceived injustices stretching from Tripoli to Baghdad and back again.

And if that's how it goes on the global scale (I haven't even mentioned the two Koreas, or China and Taiwan, or the plight of Native Americans), it works just the same on the personal level—in families, on school playgrounds, and elsewhere. Many adults can still tell you the name of the class bully or the mean-spirited teacher who made their lives miserable when they were ten years old or even younger. Many families include siblings or cousins who are "not speaking," because of something that happened years ago, perhaps decades.

The instinct for justice, in other words, runs deep. You don't have to have a master's degree in philosophical ethics to know what it's all about. It's a universal human sense: *That isn't right—something needs to be done to put it right.*

We all know it. But we all find that "putting right" is difficult. The teacher may or may not be able to sort out the problem on the playground. Parents may or may not be able to reconcile squabbling siblings. Diplomats and peacemakers may be able to bring all parties together around a table and work out agreements, but often it doesn't come off. Systems of "restorative justice" have been tried in some countries—notably New Zealand, building on elements in traditional

Maori culture. That has been creative and positive. But many countries still have "justice systems" that, seen close up, are neither just nor systematic. Here is the problem. *We all know justice matters, but we all find it difficult or sometimes downright impossible to achieve it.*

In other words, we find that *justice* serves as a signpost pointing toward what is foundational or essential to our lives. At the same time we find that it is a *broken* signpost in that, no matter how hard we strive to live up to the ideal, we fail, often in ways that create more injustice. How do we explain this tension, lying as it does at the core of so many of our problems?

A God of Justice

Those who know John's gospel well may think of it as a book about God's love, an invitation to an intimate relationship with the Father, a promise of spiritual renewal. Well, it is all those things, as we shall see. But near its heart is a message about a world held to proper account at last:

> This is the condemnation: that light has come into the
> world, and people loved darkness rather than light,
> because what they were doing was evil. For everyone who
> does evil hates the light; people like that don't come to
> the light, in case their deeds get shown up and reproved.
> But people who do the truth come to the light, so that it
> can become clear that what they have done had been done
> in God. (3:19–21)

So although many people know the famous verse in John 3:16 about how God "so loved the world" that he sent his Son to save it, they might not realize that this is followed almost immediately by this powerful statement about justice. God's light will expose the evil deeds done in darkness. Justice is a manifestation of God's love.

So the coming of God's light and love into the world is all about God's putting everything right in the end. It is about that final "passing of judgment" which, in the Jewish world, was the ultimate revelation of "justice":

> The father doesn't judge anyone, you see; he has handed over all judgment to the son, so that everyone should honor the son just as they honor the father. Anyone who doesn't honor the son doesn't honor the father who sent him.
>
> I'm telling you the solemn truth: anyone who hears my word, and believes in the one who sent me, has the life of God's coming age. Such a person won't come into judgment; they will have passed out of death into life. I'm telling you the solemn truth: the time is coming—in fact, it's here already!—when the dead will hear the voice of God's son, and those who hear it will live. You see, just as the father has life in himself, in the same way he has given the son the privilege of having life in himself. He has even given him authority to pass judgment, because he is the son of man. (5:22–27)

John's gospel, then, depicts a God who cares deeply about justice. This point is fundamental: although we humans have within ourselves a strong echo of this longing for justice, in God himself that longing is complete and perfected. Part of the hope the Christian faith offers is the knowledge that God will not allow injustice to be the last word. That is a central element in the good news of the gospel.

It is vital, then, to remember that *John's gospel is a book about how the whole world is being put right at last.* It *is* a book about justice. It tells the story of how the creator God himself is passionate about things being sorted out, straightened out. And it tells us what he has done to bring it about. Unless we read the book with this larger story in mind, we won't understand the teaching about love and comfort that we are (rightly and properly) wanting and expecting.

That ultimate truth is important for us to remember as we encounter two dark realities in John's gospel: the fact that Jesus himself is seemingly a victim of injustice, and the power of the Adversary to create and exacerbate injustice in this world.

Jesus Stands Accused

God's promises of true justice do not go unchallenged. Indeed, as the gospel story moves forward, it becomes clear that Jesus himself is, in a sense, on trial—and that this is actually good news. Some of us in this life struggle with feelings of anger, even rage, at the injustices we have suffered. Maybe we have been falsely accused. Maybe we were physically or emotionally hurt by others. One of the most redemptive messages of Christianity is that Jesus himself suffered these kinds of injustices too. This may not seem like a particularly hopeful message at first glance, but it helps us understand in the end that God is on the side of the victim—especially when we see what happens next.

Accusations and threats mount up against Jesus from early on in the Gospel of John, particularly following his healing of the lame man on the Sabbath (5:18; 7:1). These are balanced by the regular summoning of "witnesses" to testify on Jesus's behalf, including John the Baptist and then the Father himself (5:31–38). Things come to a head in chapters 7, 8, and 9 when Jesus's accusers close in, declaring that he is demon-possessed (7:20) and a "deceiver," that is, the kind of person Moses warned against in Deuteronomy, one leading the people astray (7:12). It's in this setting that Jesus again insists that right judgment is vital and will take place on God's terms:

> Don't judge by appearances! Judge with proper and right judgment! (7:24)

> You are judging in merely human terms; I don't judge anyone. But even if I do judge, my judgment is true, because I'm not a lone voice; I have on my side the father who sent me. (8:15–16)

Chapter 8 is all the more interesting because it opens with the strange little story of one particular "accusation," the attempted stoning of a woman caught in the act of adultery (8:1–11). Among the many dimensions of the story—including the extraordinary sight of Jesus squatting down and writing with his finger in the dust—we find, in particular, the question of what justice will look like in this situation.

The crowd, cynically manipulating the woman's perilous situation, is clearly hoping to frame a charge not so much against her, but against Jesus. Will he or won't he uphold the law of Moses? But, in a dramatic anticipation of the eventual playing out of the whole gospel story, Jesus turns the tables on them. "Whichever of you is without sin," he says, "should throw the first stone at her" (8:7). In other words, *he* is now accusing *them*—of both sin and hypocrisy. And they know it. They slink away, starting with the eldest. The question hangs in the air: "Where are they, woman? Hasn't anybody condemned you?" (8:10) No one has done so, and neither will Jesus.

But that question comes back with a bang in the discourse that follows. Having failed to incriminate Jesus one way, they accuse him in another, even though all the real evidence is on his side:

> "Even if I do give evidence about myself," replied
> Jesus to them, "my evidence is true, because I know
> where I came from and where I'm going to. But you
> don't know where I come from or where I'm going to.
> You are judging in merely human terms; I don't judge
> anyone."

Yes, thinks the reader; as in the story we just heard. But then he goes on:

> "But even if I do judge, my judgment is true, because I'm
> not a lone voice; I have on my side the father who sent
> me." (8:14–16)

The question Jesus asked the crowd about the woman now turns into a challenge: who is going to bring a charge of sin against *him*? (8:46). But they persist: Jesus *must* be demon-possessed (8:48, 52). By now we should see where this is going. John has transposed the question of justice, of ultimate judgment, into a different sphere. The term "the devil" in v. 44 looks back to the Hebrew term *ha-satan*, which means "the accuser," and the irony of these middle chapters in the book is that the crowds who are trying to accuse Jesus—including accusing him of being demon-possessed!—are themselves doing the work of "accusation." Hence the complexity, which will only finally be resolved at the end of the story.

At this stage what is clear is that the narrative is indeed addressing the larger question of justice, the longing of all humans that things should be put right in the end. But how? Jesus declares one more time that his whole mission is to sort things out, to clarify how everything stands:

> "I came into the world for judgment," said Jesus, "so that those who can't see would see, and so that those who can see would become blind." (9:39)

But what does this mean? And how will Jesus do this? Doesn't "justice" imply that in the end all will see and understand, even if they don't like it? And, in particular, how will the spiritual battle—since that is what is now increasingly being revealed as the real issue—be won and lost?

These questions are all interconnected. In part, the answer is, "Wait and see"—both in the sense that the drama will play out in Jesus's own trial and execution and in the larger sense that those events themselves will precipitate a new world, a new way of being, which in the longer term will lead to the ultimate new creation. But before we can get there, we have to go deeper into the dark side of the story.

The Adversary

In the light of all that has been said, we should not be surprised when finally, in chapter 12, the real "adversary" is identified. In a passage to which we shall return more than once, Jesus points to "this world's ruler" as the real culprit, the dark power behind the evil and death that has defaced and corrupted God's good world. Justice will be done at last, but not on the basis of secondary causes and agents. If John's gospel were some kind of crime novel, this would be where we would get a clear hint as to who the real villain is and how things are to be sorted out. This scene functions like a coup de théâtre, in which a director suddenly changes the lighting so that we see the real villain who had been standing in the background all along, knife poised, ready to strike.

Jesus, realizing that the moment has come, suddenly bursts out with a whole new theme. The dark power itself must be defeated if the world is to be rescued:

Now comes the judgment of this world! Now this world's ruler is going to be thrown out! And when I've been lifted up from the earth, I will draw all people to myself. (12:31–32)

This, at last, discloses how the real lawsuit now stands, how ultimate justice is going to be done. No wonder we humans can't get it right: there are larger, more shadowy forces involved. This, in other words, is not just a story about human justice. It isn't even about creation being put right, though it is that as well. It is about a dark power, a power without a real name because it is the power of anticreation. It is "the world's ruler." What has happened? How does it all fit together?

Humans have worshipped idols, and the idols have taken over. The dark force, the accuser, "the satan," the shadowy one that brings death itself, stands behind all the injustice and wickedness in the world. John is telling us that the story of Jesus—of Jesus on trial, with the witnesses lining up to give evidence and the plotters plotting against him—is the story of how the moment of judgment, the moment when the dark power will be identified and dealt with, is itself distorted—since in John's story *Jesus himself* is "identified" as the real villain and then crucified. Somehow, John is saying, this will bring about the victory of the Creator over this dark force itself. Jesus will take upon himself the judgment of God against evil.

Jesus then warns his followers that "the ruler of the world is coming" (14:30). On one level he appears to mean Rome. He is, after all, going to be facing Pontius Pilate before too long. But Pilate will simply be the mouthpiece for a suprahuman power that lives by injustice, that thrives on injustice, that embodies injustice even while claiming (as Rome did) to be bringing "justice" to the world. This is the contest at which John invites us to gaze. And this gives retrospective meaning to all the earlier hints in the story. Whose justice will win?

John begins to answer that as he sums up the first half of the story, the public career of Jesus leading up to this moment. Judgment is indeed coming. Jesus's underlying intention, to save the world, has as its necessary corollary the passing of judgment on all that is destroying it:

> If anyone hears my words and doesn't keep them, I'm not going to judge them. That wasn't why I came. I came to save the world, not to judge it. Anyone who rejects me and doesn't hold on to my words has a judge. The word which I have spoken will judge them on the last day.
>
> I haven't spoken on my own authority. The father who sent me gave me his own command about what I should say and speak. And I know that his command is the life of the coming age. What I speak, then, is what the father has told me to speak. (12:47–50)

Many who read John's gospel, I suspect, skip over passages like these. That isn't the sort of thing they want to hear. They are looking for comfort, peace, and hope—not for dark sayings about "judgment" and a strange division of labor between "the father" and "the son." Yet these sayings of Jesus are neither incidental nor accidental in John's gospel. They express something absolutely central to his purpose. If only we could glimpse how they tie things together, we would realize that they *are* about comfort, peace, and hope as well. That's what you get once the ultimate evil has itself been condemned. But all this indicates, only too clearly, the dark road that has to be trodden in order to arrive at those destinations.

Creation and New Creation

The difficulty we face in reading a book like John, to say it once more, is that it doesn't seem to match up with the story line we expect. We expect to hear about salvation, about spiritual life, about the love of God, not about judgment. And yet in any scientific or historical study, it is the bits that don't quite fit that function as the telltale signs that we need to think again. We need to revise our initial expectations in the light of what the text actually says.

John's gospel, you see, is all about *creation* and *new creation*. It is deliberately and carefully telling the story of the creator God making a good world, grieving at its collapse into wickedness and, yes, injustice, and determining to put it right. To sort it out. To do justice.

In fact, the whole gospel has been leading up to this. John's gospel is divided into two quite different sections: chapters 1–12 and 13–20, with 21 as a kind of endpiece, added (so it seems) at some point after the main book had been completed. And it all indicates that John is indeed writing about the new creation, putting the old creation right and launching the new one from the middle of the old.

John's prologue (1:1–18), which begins with a majestic, well-known introduction ("In the beginning was the Word"), echoes Genesis and Exodus, and also the Psalms and Isaiah. God's Word, which speaks creation into life, comes to "live among us" (v. 14), or to "*tabernacle* among us" (the Greek word translated "live" here, *eskēnōsen*, literally means to "pitch one's tent" or "set up camp"), like the glorious divine Presence coming to dwell in the wilderness Tabernacle (Exod. 40). John insists that the human being Jesus *is* the appropriate living revelation of the One God. He announces that the "age to come" is arriving in the present (the term "eternal life," often used in that connection, gives us the wrong impression today). Jesus therefore comes to defeat the anticreation powers that have ruled the world. The sign that he has done so comes when he inaugurates the new creation in his own physical body when he is raised from the dead. That is the story John is telling.

That is the way in which John's gospel stands in the noble Jewish tradition that refuses to allow evil and injustice to have the last word. At no point do the ancient Jewish writers throw up their hands and say, "Oh, well, there's no justice, then." They struggle on, often in the dark, trusting that the Creator cares enough about his world to set it right. And John, like all the early Jesus followers, is clear that *this is the story about how the ancient divine intention was fulfilled at last* and about how, through these events, a justice-filled world comes to birth. Now at last the possibility of setting things right comes into view.

That is one of the reasons John begins his gospel with such a clear echo of Genesis 1: "In the beginning . . ." The opening of Genesis has become a hunting ground for many people in the modern world who expect the Bible to give them "the facts" about "creation," so they can resist the attacks of rationalism ("You can't believe all that old stuff about God intervening in the world") by taking an equally rationalistic approach to the Bible ("In my Bible it says God did it like this . . ."). But such an approach often misses the point that would have leaped off the page to anyone in ancient Israel, or for that matter in ancient Rome, Greece, Egypt, or Babylon, where all kinds of different theories about the origin of the world were rife. According to the Genesis story, flying in the face of everyone else's stories, the point is that *the world was made very good, by a very good God.*

Find that hard to believe? Well, read on; things get complicated. But in the book of Genesis the ancient Israelites started to tell their own great story (the long, complex tale of Abraham and his descendants) by prefacing it with an even greater story, the story of a good God making a good world. Once they did that, then the point of Israel's story became totally bound up with the story of the good God, of his good but now flawed creation, and of his absolute and unbreakable intention to put it all right in the end. A bit like a crime novel, in fact.

The Justice Bringers

But how is it all to work out? Jesus is quite clear. One of the beautiful things that distinguishes the Christian idea of justice from others is that it is participatory: *we* are part of bringing it about. Once Jesus has done what he has to do, he will send the Spirit upon his followers, so that through our witness a new sort of justice will be born:

> When [the Spirit] comes, he will prove the world to be
> in the wrong on three counts: sin, justice, and judgment.

In relation to sin—because they don't believe in me. In relation to justice—because I'm going to the father, and you won't see me anymore. In relation to judgment—because the ruler of this world is judged. (16:8–11).

With this astonishing vision, the agenda Jesus has for his followers is *to prove the world in the wrong*. How will we do this? By following him. By being, for the world, what he was for Israel. "As the father sent me," he said after his resurrection, "so I'm sending you" (20:21). His people are sent into the world *as justice bringers*, to confront the powers that carve up the world with the news that there is a different justice and that it has already won its case.

John's description of how that case is won consists, of course, of Jesus's "trial" before Pontius Pilate, described at length in chapters 18–19. The word "justice" doesn't occur here, nor yet the word "evidence," but this is clearly where the story of the whole gospel is heading. What we are given instead are three big themes, two of which we will explore later on: kingdom, truth, and power. Once the question of justice is on the table, these are the themes we meet: who's in charge, what's the truth of the matter, and who has the power to enforce it.

Of course, it looks as though Pilate has all the cards in his hand, as indeed, from one point of view, he really does. Even Jesus recognizes this, in a breathtaking acknowledgment that the Creator really does intend that human authorities should oversee his world—to which he adds the all-important note that they will be held responsible for what they do (19:11). The multiple ironies of the whole gospel pile up, as the chief priests declare to Pilate, "We have no king except Caesar" (19:15), and as, with horrid mockery, Jesus is publicly announced as "king of the Jews" through a placard stuck above his head.

The whole point of the story, seen from this angle, is that in the crucifixion of Jesus we see the world we know—*the world where we all want justice, but where it doesn't happen.* The world where injustice wins, where the bullies and the power brokers do what they want and get away with it. The world we live in. The world into which the Incarnate Word came—to announce and to embody a different sort of justice, a justice that is "restorative" (for reasons that will become apparent), a justice in which the real source of wickedness, the dark force that stands behind the betrayal of Judas, the plotting of the chief priests, and the cynicism of the Roman governor, is first identified and allowed to do its worst and then is overcome and robbed of its power.

Resurrection Justice

All this depends, of course, on the resurrection. There are hints throughout the gospel story of a deeper justice than anyone has yet imagined, and with chapter 20 John discloses it at last. Justice is all about *creation restored,* about things being put back to rights. Only, we now see, it goes further than that. It is about *creation arriving at last at the new place for which it was made in the beginning.*

The resurrection doesn't bring us back to the Garden of Eden—though Jesus's meeting with Mary Magdalene in the garden does have distant echoes of that. It introduces us to a whole new world, a world in which death itself shall be no more.

A world in which a new kind of justice has triumphed over the old forms, the forms that, as we all know, have let us down again and again. A world in which, by the Spirit, those who follow Jesus are commissioned and equipped to be new-creation people, justice people, hope-giving people for a world where injustice still reigns.

This new creation is accomplished, in John, through Jesus's own presence, but supremely through his death, when he is "lifted up." That word, when we find it in John 12:32 and, before that, 3:14, deliberately echoes Isaiah 52:13, where the "servant" is "lifted up" and "exalted"—through being, as the following verses make clear, the victim of a cruel and unjust death. John, a master of irony as well as of Israel's scriptures, thus deliberately links the crucifixion with the revelation of divine glory.

And, as with the Bible in general, John sees the victory of God over the powers of darkness working out through actual political power and violence. In line with Isaiah 52:13–53:12, he sees Jesus's death as the moment when and the means by which that power is defeated, so that in the resurrection, the start of new creation, a new kind of power is launched upon the world. The gospel ends—particularly with the "extra" chapter (21)—with a kind of outward gaze, looking into the future. This, John is saying, is not the end of the story. It is the turning point in a much larger story. And we, the readers, are summoned to believe it and to become part of the story ourselves.

John's Jesus suffers the ultimate injustice and, with that, declares that the passion for justice that all humans feel—even though we all distort it to suit ourselves—always was a true signpost, albeit a battered and broken one, to the nature of

God. With the resurrection, the signpost has at last itself been put right. The risen Jesus has won the victory over injustice and now sends his followers to work on the multiple projects of new creation. Justice itself—restorative, healing, life-giving justice—is central to that task.

On Reading John

John's gospel is unique not only in Christian literature, but in all writings everywhere. How should we best approach it?

Think of it for a moment in terms of food. John's gospel contains all the ingredients you need for a full, first-class meal. Those who have the time (and most of us do, if we really want to) should regularly treat themselves to a sit-down, full-on, five-courses-and-wine reading of it, right through. It should take roughly a couple of hours. Take that time to savor it, to sense both its overall flow and its sudden extra flavors, its splendid nutrition and extra delights. There will always be more: more depth, more subtlety, more hints of promise.

Equally, in between long and leisured readings, John is also—if I can put it like this—a great book to snack on. I don't much like opening the Bible at random and seeing what comes up, though sometimes that does have remarkable results. But out of the whole Bible (the only other example I can think of would be the Psalms), John's gospel will reward that approach too, even while reminding you of the full meal that's waiting for you when next you have the time and the opportunity.

Even a casual glance at the New Testament will reveal that John's gospel is very different from the other three, Matthew, Mark, and Luke. They follow something of a set pattern in describing Jesus's public career and his arrival in Jerusalem a few days before his death. John has him going to and fro between Galilee and Jerusalem throughout that period. Matthew and Luke have detailed stories about Jesus's birth; John, like Mark, has none. Some of the best-loved passages in the other gospels (the Sermon on the Mount; the parable of the good Samaritan) don't occur in John; some of John's most striking moments (turning water into wine, the conversations with Nicodemus and others) are his and his alone. John's Jesus often speaks in long, somewhat rambling discourses, very different from the short, pithy sayings we mostly find elsewhere, and quite different too in both style and content from the one or two longer speeches (again, such as the Sermon on the Mount) in Matthew in particular.

Scholars have puzzled for generations as to the relationship, if any, between all four gospels. People used to think John must be later, because he seems to give us a more sharply defined view of who Jesus is (the "Word" who "becomes flesh," in other words, one who is equal with the One God of Israel and yet is a living human being). But recent work on the other three gospels indicates that they strongly agree with John on this and many other points, even though they have different ways of saying it. We are, in fact, still no closer to knowing whether John was strictly independent of the other three or whether, being familiar with one or more of them, he decided to set things out in his own way.

We are, likewise, no closer to knowing for sure when the gospels were written. They might all date from the 60s or even earlier, but equally they might derive from a decade or two later. Some still put John in the 90s, though I think that's excessive. But being "earlier" or "later," despite popular assumptions, has less to do with whether they are historically reliable. In a strongly oral culture, memories of striking incidents, particularly if they are of an extraordinary character, are told and retold. People don't forget them. The path of wisdom is to keep an open mind and heart and allow each of the four to make its impact on us as we read, whether at length or in shorter snippets.

Chapter Two

Love

I<small>F "JUSTICE" CAN FEEL COLD AND THREATENING, "LOVE"</small> always sounds warm and welcoming.

Of course, as we've said, we all know we actually need justice. We all know the world needs it. Things must to be put right, and we rejoice when that happens. But justice is necessarily impersonal. Think of the statue of the goddess Justice holding the scales—and wearing a blindfold, so she can't see who she's dealing with and is therefore deciding the case strictly on its merits. We want justice, but we don't want to live forever in a world of blindfolds. We want love.

Notoriously, the English language here has that one word where the Greeks had at least four, enabling them to distinguish easily between erotic love, affection for places or subjects, human friendship, and that generous self-giving love for which the early Christians picked up what had been a more general word, *agapē*, and gave it a new, golden meaning. People who write in English about morality or virtue often express regret for this linguistic difficulty. I have done so myself. But there is still something important to ponder about the one-word catchall "love."

The word "love," whatever its finer shades of meaning, is all about *relationship*. It is about being drawn out of myself toward something or someone else, in whatever way and with whatever short- or long-term aims or effects. It is about discovering that "I" become more fully "myself" when I am *in relationship*—even if that relationship might be, for a time at least, with a mountain, a horse, a sunset, a child, a sweetheart, a house, a hospital patient, a colleague, or a neighbor. "Love" is an arm-waving term that indicates that I know in my bones that I need to be part of something larger than myself, something that gives me a sense of coming home, something in which I find warmth, security, meaning, delight, and even a sigh of relief when that comes to expression. That is fine. It's better to wave your arms vaguely at something than to forget it exists.

Part of the problem of the modern Western world is that we *have*, by and large, forgotten it exists, although not in all ways, to be sure. Modern novels include much sensitive exploration of the different levels and dynamics of interpersonal love in relation (obviously) to sex and marriage, but also within families, villages, businesses, schools, and larger communities. These relationships are constantly investigated, deconstructed, and reassembled. Plays and poems do the same. Not long ago, skimming through a large anthology of poems looking for a suitable line, I was struck by just how much poetry emerges from the puzzles and paradoxes of love. I will come back to that.

My point is that at another level we have tried to live, to organize our corporate and individual lives, as though love was irrelevant, a pastime on the side rather than the central dynamic. This is the subject of a well-known modern myth. The story of Faust was made famous by various writers, especially the German poet Johann Wolfgang von Goethe and the novelist Thomas Mann. The story turns on the pact that Faust makes with the devil. He can have unlimited power, prestige, fame, and fortune—anything he wants at all!—but when it's all over, the devil will have his soul. And the condition, in the meantime, is that *he must not love*. It is a commentary on our times.

That is partly at least why love has struck back in other, often destructive ways. "Love of country" has been corrupted into horrific national idolatry and consequent violence. Love for a hobby or a skill can become an all-consuming obsession. "Falling in love," even when one or both parties have made lifelong promises elsewhere, is regularly deemed to justify the breaking of promises and the destruction of families. It often results, more darkly but less visibly to begin with, in the slow erosion of moral character and judgment. Having detached love from other aspects of life, it comes back all the more powerfully in less appropriate ways.

We know we need relationships at every level in order to be human. Today's rootless society, in which people change jobs and locations every few years (I speak from a lifetime of doing just that), leaves one with layers of bereavement and the constant challenge of rebuilding from scratch. Occasionally one does hear of people who appear to survive without much real human contact. Taken to extremes, that is seen as an illness. The substitution of electronic machines, smartphones, and the like for real human contact is now widely seen as a personal and social problem, though nobody seems to know what to do about it.

We know all this, I think, in our bones. We sense that something is amiss with the way things are. We want to find, as we say, "true love," not just in the often trivial sense of the ideal romance, but something that is solid, lasting, utterly reliable, and constantly life-giving. That is why, even in today's cynical world, most people love to celebrate a wedding. It appears to be raising a flag of hope in the midst of a world of broken dreams. It points to something much, much more than itself. There is an important paradox there: the deep love that has brought *these* two particular individuals together into *this* challenging and demanding commitment and relationship is not, after all, "just about them." It is about all of us. About the world. About (as John would say) God and the world. About Jesus.

We will come back to that in a moment. But, to sum up the challenge and the problem of love, we find the same thing that we found with justice. We all know it matters, matters not just like a slightly more comfortable chair or a somewhat better pair of shoes, but like fresh water to drink and clean air to breathe after making do with years of pollution. But we all find it difficult. We hurt the people we really love. Our emotions run away with us and take us to places we had no intention of going. We become obsessive. We cling to what we should renounce and turn our backs on what we should hold tightly. And even when we manage to get our "loves"—our friendships, our longings, our likings, our hobbies—in a healthy balance, they are sooner or later cruelly disrupted. Either we stand at someone else's graveside, or they stand at ours. As the bleakest of the Psalms puts it—as always, looking reality in its horrible face— "Darkness is now my only companion" (Ps. 88:18, REB).

Yet even amid all our relational brokenness, there are glimpses of hope—hope that deep, lasting, and genuine love exists and that we can be part of it. This is one way of expressing what Christian faith is all about, and John's gospel is one of the most profound statements of exactly this. This is where we see, displayed in a haunting narrative, the lengths to which the creator God will go, and the sacrifices he will make, in order to display his love in action. And behind that again we sense an even more remarkable possibility: that even God himself, in an important sense, exists "in relationship"—that love is not just something that God *does*, but the very heart of what God *is*.

To the Utmost

When we turn to John's gospel, everyone knows—well, everyone who has ever been to a church—that John talks about love. "God so loved the world that he gave his only begotten son." As millions can tell you, having been taught that verse in Sunday school, that is John 3:16. But when we say that John "talks about" love, we are only scratching the surface. John's gospel is a great love story, *the* great love story of all time. John plants love at the very center of his book. From there, it reaches out its arms to what went before and to what comes after:

> It was before the Festival of Passover. Jesus knew that his time had come, the time for him to leave this world and go to the father. *He had always loved his own people in the world; now he loved them right through to the end.* (13:1)

I love that "right through to the end." The Greek is even crisper: *eis telos*, "to the goal," "to the utmost." This isn't just about timing ("he never stopped loving them"); it's about the quality of the action. There was nothing that love could do that love did not do, that Jesus did not do. "No one has a love greater than this," he says a bit later, "to lay down your life for your friends. *You are my friends*, if you do what I tell you" (15:13–14). So that sentence in 13:1 serves as a heading for all that is to come: the betrayal by Judas, the denial by Peter, the arrest, the mocking, the trial, the callous cruelty of Calvary. When Paul wrote, in perhaps the most moving moment of his most passionate letter, that "the son of God . . . *loved me and gave himself for me*" (Gal. 2:20), he was summing up exactly the same point. Read John's whole story, from the start of chapter 13 all the way through to the end of the book, as a single, simple act of love, costing not less than everything.

Then look back to the first half of the gospel: "He had always loved his own people in the world." John is saying, as it were, "In case you hadn't realized, the entire story I have been telling you is the story of love lived out." When Jesus confronts Nicodemus and tells him about the need to be born again, this is an act of *love*. When he surprises the Samaritan woman not only by asking for a drink but by bantering with her, teasing her to the point where she does a double-take and realizes that this isn't a seduction routine but a sign of a much greater love, that Israel's Messiah is reaching out across the ugly divide to the hated "other"—this is an act of *love*. Jesus's healings and his feeding of the hungry crowd are, still more obviously, acts of love. His hard words for his angry interlocutors in chapters 7, 8, and 9 are perhaps the shadow side of love; this is what happens when love "comes to its own, and its own people do not receive it" (see 1:11).

Love then breaks out powerfully in chapter 11, though at first it seems to be denied. John tells us that Jesus loved Martha, Mary, and Lazarus—and so, when he heard that Lazarus was seriously ill, "he stayed where he was . . . for two days." The sisters later challenge him about this: "If only you'd been here," they say, "our brother wouldn't have died!" (11:6, 21, 32).

But then the extraordinary thing happens; and John, by his framing of the story in this way, is making it as clear as a good, subtle writer can that *the entire episode of the raising of Lazarus is itself an astonishing act of love*, signaling and pointing forward toward the great act of love when Jesus himself is raised from the dead. The bitter tears that Jesus cries at Lazarus's grave (11:35) and his imperious commands, "Take away the stone" and "Lazarus— come out!" are the advance equivalents of the crucifixion and resurrection. *This is what love looks like*, John is saying, *when it really goes into action*. It is always surprising, always creative, always different from the lesser vision we might have cherished.

There is more, of course—there is always more with John— and we will come back to it in a moment. But to see what it all means we have to remind ourselves what the whole book is about. What we see going on in the story of Jesus, close up and personal, is what is going on in the much larger, immeasurably larger, cosmic picture. *This is how God loves the world, his creation.*

John 3:16, then, applies to the whole book, and to the whole world. It invites us to see the entire drama of creation—the planets, the mountains, the far reaches of cosmic space, the tiniest creature on earth, the refugee, the sick child, the grieving widow, the brittle and arrogant power broker, and the creator God who made them all, loves them all, and grieves over their folly, their wickedness, and their sorrow—from this point of view. John wants us to see this whole story as being narrowed down and focused like a bright, blinding laser beam on the single human story of this man Jesus, the Word who became flesh—the flesh that reached out and touched the sick, the flesh that was nailed to a Roman cross.

John is asking us to see the story of Jesus as a huge theological balancing act. Imagine the great pyramids in Egypt. When you get up close, they are not just big; they are massive. They tower over you, solid and vast. The individual stones each weigh over two tons; since there are over two million of the stones in the largest of the pyramids, the combined weight must be nearly six million tons. Now imagine a truly enormous giant picking up one of those pyramids and turning it upside down, so that all that scary weight was resting on the one point.

That is what John's gospel is about. The whole pyramid of created life, from the physical universe itself down to the smallest creature, with human beings, vulnerable, muddled, sinful, and sorrowing, in the middle—that whole pyramid is now balanced on this one story, this one person. This is what the Creator's love looks like in action. Jesus himself, the ultimate human being, vulnerable, sorrowing, yet poised and balanced, gives himself as the embodiment of the Creator's love.

The Trinity

To speak of Jesus as "embodying" the Creator's love is to speak of "incarnation": "incarnation" is simply a Latin-based word meaning the same thing as "embodiment." But this means that John is throwing us, right from the start, into the vast mysterious depths of what theologians refer to as the Trinity. The trouble with that doctrine—and indeed the very term—is that it often appears as a challenge rather than an invitation, a puzzle rather than a welcome, something to tease the brain rather than transform the heart.

Perhaps that explains why some have suggested that the Trinity is a later idea invented by clever philosophers three or four centuries after Jesus's day, but not found in the New Testament itself. But that notion is an illusion caused by the fact that the *word* "Trinity" and the technical terms associated with it (like "person," "substance," and "nature") come later. In fact, the reality that those later words were struggling to express is woven deep and tight into the very fabric of the earliest Christian life, thought, and prayer. John's gospel provides an obvious example, but by no means the only one.

Many illustrations have been offered for how this doctrine works. Such illustrations never say everything, but they can sometimes gesture in the right direction. Think, for instance, of a vast rain-fed lake high up in the mountains. At the lake's edge is a deep cleft in the rock through which the water rushes at high speed, pouring down over the cliff to splash onto the rocks hundreds of feet below, then to be dispersed into many new streams, many channels, flowing out to irrigate a wide landscape before eventually returning to the sea. Jesus is the waterfall; the Spirit is the outflowing streams. The Father is the lake, the source, as well as the sea into which all the water flows. But the water is all the same water . . .

No, the picture isn't perfect (though water is one of John's central images for God's outpoured love), but, as I say, no illustration ever is. And actually there's a reason for this. Within Christian thought Jesus is not an *example* of something else, perhaps of a pure or abstract "principle." Jesus himself is the central reality. All theories and principles mean what they mean in relation to him. This is why the gospels matter. We can't first gain an understanding of who God might be and then try to fit Jesus into that picture. We have to do it the other way around. It is therefore only by telling and retelling the story of Jesus—and by living within that story in the power of his Spirit—that we can understand from within, as it were, what it's all about. And when we do that, we find ourselves drawn back again and again to the central point, baffling though it sounds when stated at the surface level only: the One God, the world's creator, the source and goal of all that is.

Even that language doesn't get us to the heart of it. The point (and this is why I'm emphasizing this within the present chapter) is that the followers of Jesus have always perceived and understood the true God as overflowing personal *love*. No wonder we find this hard to grasp, especially in the modern world, where "love" can easily degenerate into mere sentimentalism and so be ignored by those who want to use nothing but cold logical analysis.

Love at its best—the rich, many-sided mutual delight you find in healthy families and wider communities—is always on the move, always passing between one person and another, offering welcome to one person, consolation to another, encouragement to another, fascinated enquiry to someone else. We are who we most deeply are and we become who we most profoundly need to become through the love of others, and this love is by definition never simply a transaction, a payment for services rendered or promised. It is always a gift. That is what speaking of God as Trinity is most profoundly about.

As I said before, it isn't just that God loves—as though God did many things of which love was only one. The God we know in Jesus and the Spirit *is* love—love like that, love flowing to and fro, always between the Father and the Son, always through the Spirit, and, because this God is the creator and healer of the creation, always flowing out into the world, out into hearts and lives. The term "Trinity," at its best, is meant to evoke this glorious overflowing reality. The fact that for most people today it doesn't carry anything like that meaning is a tragedy of our times, a tragedy that John's gospel can go a long way to put right.

Love Incarnate

If we want to get right inside what John means when he speaks of Jesus embodying God's love, the best way is to reflect on what John does with the theme of the Temple. And to understand that, we need to grasp the significance of the Temple in the memory and the scriptures of the people of Israel.

Let's begin with John's most dramatic Temple scene. When Jesus enters the Jerusalem Temple, in 2:13–25, he drives out the animals and overturns the money changers' tables, disrupting the sacrificial system. The point was not simply that the animal sellers and money changers were turning his Father's house into a market, though that was true as well, as Jesus says (2:16). The point was that the Temple was now under divine judgment and was going to be replaced. This had been true half a millennium before, in Jeremiah's day, and Jesus echoes Jeremiah's warnings and promise. But this time the replacement would not be a building of bricks and mortar. The Jerusalem Temple would be replaced with a human being:

> "Destroy this Temple," replied Jesus, "and I'll raise it up in three days."
>
> "It's taken forty-six years to build this Temple," responded the Judaeans, "and are you going to raise it up in three days?" But he was speaking about the "temple" of his body. So when he was raised from the dead, his disciples remembered that he had said this, and they believed the Bible and the word which Jesus had spoken. (2:19–22)

He was speaking about the "temple" of his body. There is one of John's main clues to the meaning of his whole book, but also of the gospel as a whole. Jesus is the true Temple. He is the ultimate place where, and the means by which, the living creator God will come to live in the midst of his people, at the heart of his own creation. He will embody the living presence of the true God. He will be, so to speak, God's love enfleshed.

Many Christians in the modern world wonder why that is so important. Many have become used to thinking that you don't need buildings to worship God, and that's true. But the answer is that, throughout the Old Testament, the ultimate promise of God was not that one day he would snatch his people away from the present creation so that they could live with him somewhere else. The ultimate promise was that *he would come and live with them.* This is what divine love looks like.

Think back to the foundation story of God's people. When Moses demanded that Pharaoh release the Israelites from slavery in Egypt, the reason he gave was so that they could worship their God in the desert. Israel's God could not come to dwell among them while they were living in pagan territory, surrounded by idols and people who worshipped them. The climax of the story of the Exodus is not the crossing of the Red Sea, nor yet the giving of the Ten Commandments. These are merely preparatory. The climax is when the Tabernacle is constructed (despite nearly being cancelled by the sin of the golden calf!) and the glorious divine Presence comes to dwell in it (Exod. 40).

That moment is then recapitulated in 1 Kings 8, when Solomon dedicates the Temple in Jerusalem and the glorious divine Presence comes to dwell there. And then, after the Temple had been destroyed by the Babylonians—a catastrophe far greater than exile itself so far as Israel was concerned, since it was destroying the link between them and their God—the prophets held out the hope that one day, with a newly built and restored Temple, God would come back in glory once more. That is the promise held out in the central prophetic passage we know as Isaiah 40–55. The promise is repeated in passages like Ezekiel 43; Zechariah 1:16; 2:10–11; and Malachi 3:1. But nobody in that postexilic period or subsequently said that it had actually happened. Until now.

The idea of God dwelling amid his people has two spin-off themes in the Old Testament, both of which are picked up (and transformed) in the New. The first is the close link between temple and king. David declares his intention to build a "house" for God, but God responds by saying that he, God, will build a "house" for David—meaning not a building of stone and timber (David already has one of those), but a *family* (2 Sam. 7:1–17). It might look as though God had just changed the subject, but that's wrong. This is God saying that, though at the moment he is indeed allowing his glory to dwell in a mobile tabernacle—and he will graciously allow David's son (Solomon) to build him a permanent residence—it would ultimately be far more appropriate for him to dwell with his people *in and as a human being, and that human being would be David's great coming Son.* This makes sense within the wider culture. In subsequent Jewish tradition, as in many surrounding cultures, royalty and temple building went together.

Jesus's claim about the Temple and his body in John 2, then, must be read in view of this link between king and temple. We have already been told, at the end of chapter 1, that people were seeing Jesus as the coming Messiah. Some might naturally interpret that as indicating that Jesus was going to build or restore the Temple. John sees it as meaning that he would *be* the Temple.

The point of this should be obvious to anyone who has been told, as many of us were when we were younger, that the idea of "incarnation"—of the One God becoming *human*, of all things—makes no sense. It makes no sense, people used to tell us, for God to shrink himself into a human form, with all that this would involve (I had an email just the other day from someone asking how I could possibly think of God going to the bathroom and that sort of thing). To look at it the other way around, if a human being, *any* human being, thought that he or she was "God," that person would surely be deemed crazy; that sort of thinking would be on a level with believing oneself to be a football or a piece of cheese.

But this objection fails to reckon with the way the Temple was always seen. Read the Psalms: in them the creator of the universe is said to have chosen to set up permanent residence on the little hill to the southeast of the small city called Jerusalem. If that makes sense, incarnation makes sense—only more so. In Israel's scriptures, humans were made *in the image of God*, so that if God were going to "become" anything, then becoming *human* would be utterly appropriate, in the way it would not be appropriate for him to become an elephant or a cactus.

In every other temple in the ancient world, the most important thing in the building was precisely an *image* of the god, placed in the innermost shrine. Worshippers could draw near to the deity by worshipping the image; the power of the deity would resonate out into the surrounding world. There was no image in the Jerusalem Temple, because the Israelites had been forbidden one. Humans, living humans, were the "image." That meant, in some traditions, a special focus on the king or the high priest; these figures were the humans through whom God's saving, protecting, sanctifying presence would become a reality. Now here in John we have Jesus as the truly human one *who is the Word made flesh.* You can't fit this idea into a modern Western worldview. But when you understand how first-century Jews might think, it makes complete sense.

That is why, in the climactic verse in John's prologue, we read that the Word became flesh *and "tabernacled" among us* (1:14). This is where the echoes of Genesis in John 1:1 ("In the beginning . . .") reach forward and translate into echoes of Exodus. The creator God has come to enact the new Exodus and has therefore set up camp in the midst of his people in the person of Jesus, the creative Word through whom all things were made. He is the Messiah. He is the Image. He is the Word made flesh. By drawing attention to all this in the first two chapters, John has given us the decisive clue for understanding Jesus himself and what the One God was doing in and through him, all firmly anchored in the thinking and the symbolic system of the first-century Jewish world.

I said there were two things to notice about the Temple, the first of which was the intimate link with David's son. The second—hinted at here and there in Israel's scriptures, but coming through strongly in the New Testament—is that the living presence of God in the Tabernacle or the Jerusalem Temple was sometimes seen as a signpost to what God intended for the entire creation. The Tabernacle and the Temple were never supposed to be a retreat *away* from the world, a safe hiding place while the world went to hell. They were a bridgehead *into* the world, an advance down payment on what God would do one day with all creation. Now, in John, Jesus himself is the true Temple, the place where YHWH's glory has come to dwell ("The Word became flesh, and lived among us; we gazed upon his glory," 1:14). Through his work, his death, and then particularly his resurrection, Jesus is in himself the beginning of the fulfillment of that worldwide promise.

"I Lay Down My Life for the Sheep"

The Gospel of John hinges upon the actions of one truly remarkable human being who gives himself in utter love to his friends and followers. This is the foundation of what it means to love us right through to the end, and it undergirds many scenes in the body of the book, including the image of Jesus as the Good Shepherd. When we hold these vivid, deeply human pictures in mind, we realize the full import of what is being said:

> I am the good shepherd. I know my own sheep, and my own know me—just as the father knows me and I know the father. And I lay down my life for the sheep. . . . My sheep hear my voice. I know them, and they follow me. I give them the life of the coming age. They will never, ever perish, and nobody can snatch them out of my hand. My father, who has given them to me, is greater than all, and nobody can snatch them out of my father's hand. I and the father are one. (10:14–15, 27–30).

Yes, we think, looking back through the gospel. That's what's been going on, and that's where it is all leading. And what we are witnessing as we look at this man, creative, teasing, loving, stern, the master of the situation though never in the manner people might have expected—what we are seeing is *the true reflection and embodiment of the Father himself.* That is what John is asking us to believe, and the closer attention we pay to his gospel, the more sense it makes. The detailed, personal concern and the creative, self-giving love that Jesus lavishes on everyone, with his trademark combination of a light touch and a deeply serious intent, is what it looks like when the Creator himself comes to be with us, to "pitch his tent" in our midst.

You can imagine people looking at Jesus, listening to something he said—and then looking back, straight into his eyes, and realizing that, underneath the easy manner and light tone, *he really means it.* He is telling the truth. And you start to realize what John, perhaps above all, wants us to get into our heads and our hearts—the utter *appropriateness* of the Incarnation. It wasn't a category mistake for the Word to become flesh. What, after all, did we think the Creator was like? Like a huge blob of heavenly gas? Like a distant, faceless Managing Director? Or—like Jesus?

All this propels us forward into the passage we call the Farewell Discourses, Jesus's long talk with his followers after the Last Supper. John introduces it with the story many have seen as itself a deliberate advance sign, a typical prophetic "acted parable," of what Jesus was about to do in going to his death. This is what love looked like that night.

It was suppertime. The devil had already put the idea of betraying Jesus into the heart of Judas, son of Simon Iscariot. Jesus knew that the Father had given everything into his hands and that he had come from God and was going to God. So he got up from the supper table, took off his clothes, and wrapped a towel around himself. Then he poured water into a bowl and began to wash the disciples' feet and wipe them with the towel he was wrapped in . . .

So when he had washed their feet, he put on his clothes and sat down again.

"Do you know what I've done to you?" he asked. "You call me 'teacher' and 'master,' and you're right. That's what I am. Well then: if I, as your master and teacher, washed your feet just now, you should wash each other's feet. I've given you a pattern, so that you can do things in the same way that I did to you." (13:12–15)

An example to follow? Yes, of course, in every sphere of life into which the image of foot washing can be "translated." But also a sign of what was to come. We are here very close to Paul's poetic portrait of Jesus:

> Who, though in God's form, did not
> regard his equality with God
> as something he ought to exploit.
> Instead, he emptied himself,
> and received the form of a slave,
> being born in the likeness of humans.
> And then, having human appearance,
> he humbled himself, and became
> obedient even to death,
> yes, even the death of the cross. (Phil. 2:6–8)

And the purpose of this love-in-action was *to make his people clean.* He had already promised, strangely, that the Spirit would be poured out on his followers (7:39). We will get to that in more detail in the next chapter. But John had indicated that this could not happen until Jesus had been "glorified," that is, until he had been lifted up on the cross. The foot washing points ahead to the ultimate act of self-giving, self-humiliating love on the cross, through which Jesus's followers are made clean, so that like the Temple itself they are fit places for the Spirit to come and dwell and, through that indwelling, made able in the wider world to love as Jesus had loved them.

The Farewell Discourses, which follow the foot-washing scene, are all in one way or another about love, the real, deep, practical love that Jesus himself exemplified and lived out. We should not forget the context, about which John is very clear. All this takes place as Judas, indwelt by the spirit of the "Accuser," "the satan," goes off to "accuse" Jesus, to arrange for the posse of soldiers who will come to arrest him. The better we understand what John is saying, summing up here the entire narrative of Israel's scriptures, the better we will grasp the fact that when the project of ultimate love, covenant love, divine creative love, is going ahead, the dark forces of evil will do their worst. Whether we understand it or not—whether we *like* it or not, which mostly we don't and won't—what love has to do is not only to face misunderstanding, hostility, suspicion, plotting, and finally violence and murder, but somehow, through that whole horrid business, to draw the fire of ultimate evil onto itself and to exhaust its power.

This is where we realize that the Faustian pact by which an individual or a whole culture can give up "love" in order to gain "power" is an exercise in ultimate, world-destroying futility. Love itself is the most powerful thing, because it is love that takes the worst that evil can do and, absorbing it, defeats it. That is what John is saying throughout chapters 13–19. That is what he wants us to be thinking as we read his story of Jesus before Pilate, of Jesus going to his death, of Jesus on the cross taking final thought for his mother and his close, younger friend (19:25–27).

That too is what Jesus's followers are supposed to be doing, from that moment onward. This is where, as with an icon, just when we think we are looking at something else, we find that it is looking back at us:

I'm giving you a new commandment, and it's this: love one another! Just as I have loved you, so you must love

one another. This is how everybody will know that you
are my disciples, if you have love for each other. (13:34–35)

"If anyone loves me," Jesus replied, "they will keep
my word. My father will love them, and we will come
to them and make our home with them. Anyone who
doesn't love me won't keep my word. And the word
which you hear isn't mine. It comes from the father, who
sent me." (14:23–24)

The story John has told, then, is the story of a love that answers
the longing and resolves the puzzlement we sketched earlier. John's
gospel says a clear, no-nonsense *yes* to the longing, the desire, the
anguish of our broken and messed-up loves, our obsessions, and
our self-absorption. Yes, that is (our distortion notwithstanding),
to the reality that as God-reflecting human beings *we are made for
love*, made to find ourselves in and through love, the love we give
and the love we receive.

But John is totally clear that this love, embodied and dramatically lived out by Jesus himself in his utter seriousness and
light-touch playfulness, comes to us through, and only through,
the victory won on the cross over the dark distortions. It comes
to us as part of new creation. The resurrection says God's *yes* to
the whole created order and, with it, to the love that all humans
know in their bones is central to what it means to *be* human.
The love that Jesus's followers are then called to offer to one
another and to the world—the love that is, as Paul says, the first
element of the "fruit of the spirit"—this love is public truth.
When the world sees it, it will recognize it as the genuine article.

That too will not work "automatically." It will have much

the same effect as Jesus's own work: he came to his own, and his own people didn't receive him. The fact that the gospel of Jesus and the power of the Spirit really do answer the deepest questions of human life doesn't mean that people will necessarily want those answers. But they will be true. And they will open the door to that multidimensional human life we refer to, loosely, by the term "spirituality."

God's Covenant Love in John's Scriptural Imagination

I commented earlier on the way in which the English word "love" has become broad and imprecise. Within the scripture-reading traditions to which John and the other early Jesus followers obviously belonged, "love" had a very particular meaning. It was focused on the "covenant" between God and Israel—and on the ultimate purposes of that covenant. Thus:

> It was not because you were more numerous than any other people that YHWH set his heart upon you and chose you—for you were the fewest of all peoples. It was because YHWH loved you and kept the oath that he swore to your ancestors, that YHWH has brought you out with a mighty hand, and redeemed you from the house of slavery. (Deut. 7:7–8)

This covenant generates a powerful sense of obligation: those whom the One True God loves like this must love him—in other words, remain loyal to him and cherish their relationship with him above everything else—in return:

> Know therefore that YHWH your God is God, the faithful God who maintains covenant loyalty with those who love him and keep his commandments, to a thousand generations. (Deut. 7:9)

This theme is reflected sorrowfully when Israel notably fails in these obligations:

> When Israel was a child, I loved him, and out of Egypt I called my son. The more I called them, the more they went from me; they kept sacrificing to the Baals, and offering incense to idols. (Hos. 11:1–2)

Like a grieving father, Israel's God reflects on the tragedy in terms of love given and spurned:

> Yet it was I who taught Ephraim to walk, I took them up in my arms; but they did not know that I healed them. I led them with the cords of human kindness, with bands of love. . . . How can I give you up, Ephraim? How can I hand you over, O Israel? (Hos. 11:3–4, 8)

The prophet Jeremiah names this faithful love as the reason that God will ultimately renew the covenant with Israel:

> Thus says YHWH: . . . I have loved you with an everlasting love; therefore I have continued my faithfulness to

you . . . for I have become a father to Israel, and Ephraim is my firstborn. (Jer. 31:2–3, 9)

The great prophecies collected together in the book we call Isaiah reflect the same unshakeable divine love in messages of hope, in whole chapters like Isaiah 43 and in reflections upon the original Exodus event such as we find in 63:9:

It was no messenger or angel, but his presence that saved them; in his love and in his pity he redeemed them; he lifted them up and carried them all the days of old.

And this love will win the victory, even over the necessary dislocation caused by Israel's rebellion and wickedness:

For a brief moment I abandoned you, but with great compassion I will gather you. In overflowing wrath for a moment I hid my face from you, but with everlasting love I will have compassion on you, says YHWH, your Redeemer. . . . For the mountains may depart and the hills be removed, but my steadfast love shall not depart from you, and my covenant of peace shall not be removed, says YHWH, who has compassion on you. (Isa. 54:7–8, 10)

This is all the more significant for our understanding of John, since when he introduces his book with the dramatic line, "In the beginning was the Word," among the passages he is evoking is the theme of God's powerful, rescuing, re-creative Word in Isaiah 40–55 (see particularly 40:8; 55:11).

All in all, then, the biblical theme of divine love, which John has inherited and which he sees coming to dramatic and personal fresh expression in Jesus, is not simply a generalized statement that the Creator of the universe is benevolent rather than indifferent or hostile. The divine love has to do, much more specifically, with God's choice of Abraham and his family as his beloved people, his "covenant partners," as some have put it. But the relationship has been disrupted: Israel has been unfaithful, and the result has been the catastrophe of exile—as Deuteronomy itself had always warned. That theme too comes to a dark fulfillment in John's gospel, especially in the figures of Judas and Peter; and, as John says in the prologue, Jesus came to what was his own, and his own people did not accept him.

The overarching theme of God's powerful covenant love is, of course, the reason betrayal is so devastating. John makes that quite clear as well. But the answer to betrayal (as with Judas) or denial (as with Peter) is simply a further outpouring of love. This simply reinforces our sense of gratitude that the creator God, revealed in Jesus and now active in the Spirit, does not simply love us when we are lovable, but loves us all the more—gives his very life for us, in fact—when we are horribly unlovable. That is what Paul meant when he said, "The Messiah died for us while we were still sinners" (Rom. 5:8). It is what John meant when he wrote that famous line about God "so loving the world" (3:16).

Now, however, the covenant is going to be renewed. The divine love, acting powerfully through the divine Word, will come in person to rescue God's people and, with them, the larger worldwide purpose for which they were called in the first place. That is exactly the story John is telling. Only now we know the human name of the Word—and, with that, we see the human face of the divine Love.

Chapter Three

Spirituality

S PIRITUALITY" WASN'T A WORD ANYBODY MUCH USED
in my younger days. I remember when I first heard it and,
realizing the job it was doing, I saw at once that it was going
to be useful. The fact that until perhaps the late 1960s or early
1970s it wasn't a category people needed to talk about tells you
something about the journey our culture has been on.

The 1960s were, in fact, a time of enormous transition in
Western culture. In the 1950s things had been relatively quiet.
With the war over at last, that generation heaved a sigh of relief, went back to ordinary life, and did its best to put the world
back the way people remembered. But the forces of change
were rumbling away, and the baby-boomer generation—my
generation—became teenagers and then twenty-somethings in
the 1960s and decided to get rid of some of the old patterns of
life.

One of the things that went out of the window for many of my contemporaries was "religion." In the 1950s plenty of people in Britain still went to church; rapid decline set in during the 1960s (though there were then, as there still are, many thriving churches). It was more about a mood, a feeling in the air, that all that old fusty "religion" (chilly churches, boring sermons, hopeless music) was "old hat" and nobody serious bothered with it anymore. In my younger days the leaders of the Labour Party would attend the local Methodist church during the annual Party Conference and be invited to read the Bible passages during the worship service. By the 1970s that had long gone, never to return. Until that time, as well, major sporting events were not held on Sundays. It was assumed that people wanted Sunday to be different. Some might well want to go to church. That too is long gone.

The situation in America has been very different, but what some have loosely called the process of secularization is well underway there now and seems to be spreading. So when people say today that they're not "religious," I think this is what they mostly mean. "Religion" is for yesterday's people—but "spirituality" is on the move.

This difference was marked even within official expressions of Christianity itself. In early 1969, at the height of the hippie revolution, the college chaplains in Oxford organized a "mission." The main speaker was the then Bishop of Durham, Ian Ramsey—a fine philosopher and a fine speaker. His talks were interesting, but not compelling. Audiences wobbled and slumped. But the backup speaker was Metropolitan Anthony Bloom, the Russian Orthodox archbishop in exile. He was different.

A few dozen attended the first of his "school of prayer" sessions one lunchtime. The next day the venue was packed. Thereafter, if I remember rightly, his talks had to be moved into a larger space. And, to the surprise and alarm of some, he voluntarily planted himself outside one of the great buildings in central Oxford at 11 a.m., when students were going to and fro between lectures. He stood there in his cassock, with his great Russian beard and his eyes like bottomless pools, and talked, in a steady, quiet voice, about God. Crowds gathered and forgot their lectures. I think what we witnessed in that week was the emphatic decline of "religion" and the sudden interest in "spirituality."

The narrative of "religion" and "spirituality"—for which I have focused on the 1960s partly because I remember the moment well and partly because I do believe that was a turning point for much of Western culture—has a backstory and a "forward story" as well. From the eighteenth century onward popular Western culture has largely relegated "religion" to the private sphere. This has allowed many aspects of social, public, and political life to proceed on the basis of a "functional atheism." God is out of the picture—he seems to have retired to an upstairs attic and hasn't been seen for quite some time—so we can get on with running the world downstairs without him. And we don't need religion to do that.

But "spirituality"? Well, that's something different. Henry Ford claimed in his autobiography that in 1909, when he put his Model T up for sale, he offered customers "any color you like, as long as it's black." For a great many people today you can have "any variety of spirituality you like, as long as it's *not Christian*."

So in place of the traditional Christian faith and practice in Europe and America—varied and checkered though it had been—there came the worship of other gods such as sex, money, and power. And today we see a rehabilitation of forms of "gnosticism." This ancient philosophy—which took then, and takes now, many different forms—proposes that what matters about humans is a secret inner core, a "real self," which needs to be identified and allowed to express itself. This is often a "self" quite different from the "outer person."

This philosophy was popular in the second and third centuries, not least among Jewish groups and some on the edge of the Christian faith, who had given up hope for God-driven change in the real world and had turned inward instead. It was never a religion of *redemption*, in which God had to step in and rescue people—except in the sense that God might ultimately take you away from the present world altogether. It was always a religion of *self-discovery*. A "revealer" figure might be able to show you that you were actually a spark of light from another world (or whatever).

Gnosticism in the second century, and also in the twentieth and twenty-first, has been a way of escaping from the dangers of political oppression. Empires that might object if you thought through what it meant that there was only One God and that Jesus was the world's true Lord would give you no trouble if you said that you were pursuing a quest of inner enlightenment and ultimate otherworldly salvation. As many have pointed out, some form of gnosticism has been the default mode for many Americans for a long time, as witnessed by the many movies whose theme is "finding who I really am." The entire world of "virtual reality" has a clear gnostic tinge to it, and we see every day how social media enables people to invent, then project, and then try to live up to a persona that is significantly different from their real, whole, messy, and muddled self.

We could go on exploring these themes quite easily simply by collecting an armful of books from the "mind-body-spirit" section of the average bookshop. But the point will by now be obvious. There are a great many people in today's world who do *not* think of themselves as either "religious" or indeed "Christian," but who *do* think of themselves as somehow "spiritual." Back to Henry Ford: any kind of spirituality, as long as isn't "religious." Particularly *as long as it's not Christian*, the thinking goes.

Yet Christianity speaks uniquely to the broken signpost that is spirituality. As we shall now see, God answers our longing for spiritual connection by interjecting glimpses of heaven on earth. That is what the Jerusalem Temple was all about, and for John that was what Jesus was all about. Nor does the fresh vision of spirituality stop there. God calls us to active participation, to a new life that is both God's gift and a deeply humanizing power, a new breath within us. In John's vision, the often puzzling quest for spirituality, the need to know and be known at the deepest levels, is fulfilled at last.

Temple and Torah

So what might John's gospel say to our questions about spirituality? How does this broken signpost look in the light of John's story of Jesus?

I think John would be surprised and puzzled—and deeply disappointed—at the sheer amount of muddled thinking in Europe and America over the last two or three hundred years. The fixed points in his world were quite different from those in ours (and I'm not talking about our modern scientific knowledge, space travel, and so forth). But when it comes to spirituality, we in our world have the same choices that were available in the ancient pagan world. Either the gods are largely absent (Epicureanism); they are somehow divine forces within us and the world (Stoicism); they live in a nonphysical and nontemporal world to which our souls can escape (Platonism); or they are particular forces operating in different areas of life (ordinary paganism). John, however, lived in the Jewish world, which was as radically different then as it is radically different now. For Jews, the One God of creation was utterly *different* from the world, and yet *intimately involved* with it.

That paradox (God as completely "other than" the world, yet closely involved with it) is second nature to the Psalmists. It is basic to the Prophets. It is the main subject of the "Five Books," the Torah of Moses. *And it finds its principal expression in the Temple*, the place where heaven and earth came together. Of course, as Solomon said in 1 Kings 8:27, heaven and the highest heaven couldn't *contain* the creator God of all the earth. But God had promised to come and dwell with his people, and under the right circumstances that is what he did.

This was, to put it mildly, a highly dangerous proposition. Everyone in the ancient world knew that to come face-to-face with the living God—if such an event could really happen—could be devastating. That's why, right after the story of the setting up of the Tabernacle and God's coming to live there, we find a whole book (Leviticus) devoted to what we might call health and safety regulations focusing on the regular sacrificial rites and other cultic practices designed to ensure purity, so that God would indeed dwell with his people. That's why, when Isaiah had his vision of God himself in the Temple (6:1–13), he assumed his last moment had come. And it is why nobody except the high priest himself, and then only one day a year, was allowed into the inner sanctum of the Temple, the Holy of Holies. That day was the Day of Atonement, when the high priest went in there precisely to make atonement for the accumulated sins of the people: to ensure that God would stay with them, would not leave them. It had happened before (Ezek. 1–10).

So the Temple was the center of what we might call (though they did not) ancient Israelite "spirituality." If God was dwelling in their midst, what greater delight, what more transformative experience, could there be than to be there close by him, to sense his powerful and loving presence? "Happy are those who live in your house," says the Psalmist, "ever singing your praise" (84:4). The poet can't imagine anything better than being there and worshipping God all day long.

But though the Temple was central, by the time of the Second Temple period (roughly the last four centuries BC and the first century AD), after the Babylonian exile, the other key element from the book of Exodus was seen as equally vital. This was Torah, the Five Books of Moses. Those books form a narrative of the great story of the One God and his people, which at the end of Deuteronomy continued on to "the latter days," in which the Jews of Jesus's day believed themselves to be living. But Torah was increasingly seen as the book of instruction, the law code that regulated all aspects of Jewish life. (If it appeared not to mention some particular point, it could be teased into supplying the relevant instruction by the learned scribes and teachers whose delight it was to make sure that Torah would in fact apply to all of life.)

The reason for this is not hard to find, since it too is there in the Psalms. All of life is to become a prayer, a glad self-offering. Whether you are in the Temple or far away, if Torah is in your heart and mind, you will be worshipping God just as much as the lucky ones in the Jerusalem Temple itself:

> The law of YHWH is perfect, reviving the soul;
> The decrees of YHWH are sure, making wise the
> simple;
> The precepts of YHWH are right, rejoicing the heart;
> The commandment of YHWH is clear, enlightening
> the eyes;
> The fear of YHWH is pure, enduring forever;
> The ordinances of YHWH are true and righteous
> altogether.
> More to be desired are they than gold, even much
> fine gold;
> Sweeter also than honey, and drippings of the
> honeycomb. (Ps. 19:7–10)

This passage forms part of a poem—the British writer C. S. Lewis hailed it as one of the finest poems ever written—whose earlier part celebrates the goodness of creation, reflecting upon the way in which the natural order, particularly the heavens and the sun itself, declares the goodness of the Creator. The sun's light and heat, says the poet, reach into every corner of the world—and *that's exactly what Torah does with us*, he says. That's the point of the poem. Torah acts in the human being like the sun in the world, bringing life, wisdom, joy, light, fortitude, truth, and even such a sense of sweetness that would put the honeybees out of business.

It has been customary in many Western Christian traditions to see "Jewish legalism" as a negative form of "religion," an attempt to keep a bunch of strange moral laws in a vain effort to please God with "good works." That danger was just as well known by wise teachers in Jesus's day as it is in our own. And their relentless and detailed application of Torah to every aspect of life had nothing whatever to do with that kind of low-grade self-serving spirituality. They were simply following through on what Psalm 19 had said. (We might note that Psalm 119 says similar things, only at much greater length.)

The point is that the God of Israel didn't just want to live in the midst of his people in the Temple. His desire was that his very life, his breath of life, wisdom, joy, and so on would be *inside their very individual selves*. After all, if they really were made in his image, what could be more appropriate than for that image to come to life and vividly express the reality of God's power and love in a life that is both truly human and truly God-reflecting and becoming more and more so all the time?

We note that these two focal points of ancient Jewish spirituality, Temple and Torah, are deeply *affirmative of creation*, celebrating its goodness, while equally refusing to worship it. The point of both is that God's people, Israel, are called to a genuine human existence, and that this genuine, image-bearing humanness is attained in close relation with the living God, in physical proximity through the Temple and in inner life through the Torah. This is what the biblical tradition offers as true spirituality, which all humans know in their bones they want but which our regular attempts at so often fail to attain. John can explain why that happens.

Jesus as the New Temple

John's gospel picks up these two images, Temple and Torah. He has understood exactly what they are all about. They are the very center of a rich Jewish spirituality, the likes of which you would never guess from ordinary paganism or from the philosophical alternatives. John has brought them into startling fresh reality. For him, they are about Jesus and the Spirit.

This becomes explicit in chapter 2, where (as we saw in the previous chapter) Jesus speaks of the Temple's destruction and rebuilding, and John comments, "He was speaking about the 'temple' of his body" (2:21). Jesus is the reality—the living presence of the One God right there in their midst—for which even the great Jerusalem Temple was simply an advance signpost. John is thereby declaring that in Jesus we have the long promised personal presence of Israel's God. Of course, as in 1 Kings 8, everybody knows that God himself cannot be contained by even the highest heaven; he condescends to dwell in the Jerusalem Temple. The paradox of the Incarnation—that there is One God, known now as Father and Son—is simply the full and final version of the Temple paradox. And that in turn is the paradox of grace, of the way in which the sovereign Lord of all creation comes in both a blaze of glory and a gentle touch. As Isaiah 40:1–11 puts it, at the start of the great poem of restoration, YHWH comes in triumph so that the hills will be flattened before him and the valleys filled in; and yet he comes to lead his people like a shepherd who takes care of the lambs and the mother sheep.

For John, then, Christian spirituality is focused on Jesus himself, on the presence of Jesus during his public career and on the continuing presence of the risen, ascended, and very much alive Jesus thereafter. He is to be believed, worshipped, trusted, obeyed, and followed. Those who even begin this path find that, as for the Psalmist in the Temple, being in this rich Presence is the fullness of joy. Singing his praises is daily delight. Getting to know him in word (reading the four gospels) and sacrament (the joy of the church at every baptism, every bread breaking) is like an ever-increasing intimacy with a close friend, family member, or spouse.

This intimacy comes with a relational gift attached. In John 1:12, we learn that those who accept Jesus, who "believe in his name," discover that through him they themselves become "God's children." This is one of the great biblical designations for God's people, specifically at the time of the Exodus (Exod. 4:22), which John echoes in so many ways. As John's gospel moves forward, we gradually discover how this happens—through the work of the Spirit, whom Jesus is promising to his followers (7:39; 20:22). Those who believe in Jesus and follow him are themselves to become "little temples," places where the One God truly dwells.

Vine and Branches

The most vivid Johannine expression of the relationship between Jesus and his followers comes in chapter 15, when Jesus speaks of himself as the "vine" and his friends as the "branches." The "vine" is a biblical image for the people of Israel; Jesus is insisting that with him, as Israel's Messiah, the destiny of God's people is now at last fulfilled. There was a carved vine on the Temple in Jesus's day, and here Jesus is describing the relationship his followers are to have with him in a way that says, in effect, *This is now the replacement for the intimate closeness you would have with Israel's God in the Temple*:

> "I am the true vine," said Jesus, "and my father is the gardener. He cuts off every branch of mine that doesn't bear fruit; and he prunes every branch that does bear fruit, so that it can bear more fruit. You are already clean. That's because of the word that I've spoken to you.
>
> "Remain in me, and I will remain in you! The branch can't bear fruit by itself, but only if it remains in the vine. In the same way, you can't bear fruit unless you remain in me. I am the vine; you are the branches. People who remain in me, and I in them, are the ones who bear plenty of fruit. Without me, you see, you can't do anything.
>
> "If people don't remain in me, they are thrown out, like a branch, and they wither. People collect the branches and put them on the fire, and they are burned. If you remain in me, and my words remain in you, ask for

whatever you want, and it will happen for you. My father is glorified in this: that you bear plenty of fruit, and so become my disciples." (15:1–8)

Here we see an intimate relationship between Jesus and his followers that is rooted in the ultimate intimacy between the Father and the Son and worked out through the Spirit. John is quite clear where it should all lead—to the rich, multilayered but unbreakable unity of Jesus's disciples (chap. 17). We would be right to see Jesus's prayer for the unity of his followers as another facet, perhaps the most telling one, of the love spoken of in 13:1.

This closeness lies at the heart of the Farewell Discourses (John 13–17), which we noticed in the last chapter, but about which something further must now be said. Anyone who is used to reading the gospel story the way Mark tells it, where Jesus arrives in Jerusalem at last and goes into the Temple to enact prophetically its forthcoming destruction, might be puzzled on reading the order of events in John's gospel. John's "triumphal entry" scene, not unlike the one described by Mark (12:12–19) and, for that matter, by Matthew and Luke as well, occurs in chapter 12, but Jesus's disruption of Temple practices has already occurred in chapter 2.

But now we see, perhaps, what John has done in placing that incident at the start. This time, Jesus comes to Jerusalem; teaches, prays, and warns about what is going to happen; and then takes the disciples to the upper room, where he speaks about the intimate (and very demanding) relationship they have with him and how this is to be effected. *Jesus's foot washing, his talking with his disciples in the upper room, and his prayer for their unity and witness are the new equivalent of the Temple.* This is what it means for them to be near him, just as worshippers in Israel's Temple found themselves near to Israel's God. John has woven the theology and spirituality he is advocating—in which Jesus is the true Temple and his followers are the worshippers within that Temple—into the very structure of his story.

John's Temple theology emerges in full glory in chapter 17, which has often been spoken of as the High-Priestly Prayer. Jesus prays to the Father with his followers on his heart, just as Aaron and his sons prayed for Israel in the presence of Israel's God. This completes the circle of the Farewell Discourses: cleansing at the start (chap. 13); prayer at the conclusion (chap. 17); and in between that closeness of relationship with Jesus himself that is the very heart of Christian spirituality (chap. 15). That vision of a richly biblical and rehumanizing spirituality sums up what John would have to say to our puzzled attempts today.

John's vision comes to expression particularly in the language of friendship. Friendship was a major topic of discussion among ancient philosophers, but here John seems to highlight it as a way of shifting the idea of "Temple worshippers" into the new mode, the new life that consists of Jesus himself and his followers. "I'm not calling you 'servants' any longer," he says. "Servants don't know what their master is doing. But I've called you 'friends,' because I've let you know everything I heard from my father" (15:15).

As we saw earlier, John has given us throughout the gospel a taste of what it might mean to be a "friend" of Jesus. (Some of today's teachers of Christian spirituality make much of the idea of being Jesus's "friend," and that is fully appropriate—providing we take it in the full biblical sense rather than the casual modern sense of a friend as "someone I vaguely know and quite like.") In his easy, relaxed yet challenging and demanding relationships with his first followers in chapter 1, with his mother in chapter 2, with Nicodemus and the Samaritan woman in chapters 3 and 4 (we will come back to them presently), with the disciples again and again, discussing what to do and coping with their misunderstandings (chaps. 6, 10), Jesus is present, he is real, he can be talked to—and he will talk back. Indeed, he will initiate conversations, sometimes bringing up topics we might want to shy away from, as happens in his embarrassing exchange with Peter in chapter 21.

That, no doubt, is why many generations of Christian readers have found John's gospel such a help as they take their first steps in getting to know Jesus for themselves. This book is full of tips on "how to be a friend of the Living Word," the eternal Word who has become and remains fully and gloriously human—and who clearly enjoys it, enjoys being with his friends, engaging with them as they pray, as they study scripture, as they wash one another's feet (literally and metaphorically), as they find fresh infusions of his life, his very lifeblood, in the bread and wine (chap. 6).

This playful and life-giving interchange comes into final focus in the conversations between the risen Jesus and three of his followers in the remarkable "resurrection" chapters 20 and 21. Mary thinks he is the gardener. Thomas wants to touch and see. Peter needs to know he has been forgiven for his triple denial. We will look at these marvelous short scenes later on. For the moment we merely comment that they, like those earlier scenes, carry the same utterly loving combination of deep seriousness and light touch. One can imagine the smile playing around Jesus's lips as he speaks Mary's name or as he says to Thomas, "All right—if that's what you want. Bring your finger on over. Let's do it!" One can imagine the lead weight in Peter's heart when Jesus asks, "Do you love me?" and the astonishing lightness as Jesus then says, "Feed my lambs. Look after my sheep. Feed my sheep" (21:15–17).

The center of Johannine spirituality, then, is the replacement of the Temple by Jesus himself. But that isn't the end of the story. The surprising next phase is that, if Jesus is the true Temple, *his followers are to be Temple people too.* The living God is going to make his home, as Jesus promised, not just *with* them, but actually *in* them. They—we—are the branches, extending out into the world, brought to life by God's Spirit so that we too can feed the lambs and tend the mother sheep.

Living as Reborn

One of the most striking promises in John's gospel, answering directly today's confusions about spirituality, concerns the coming of the Spirit. At the Festival of Tabernacles Jesus shouts out an invitation, like the invitation at the start of Isaiah 55: "If anybody's thirsty, they should come to me and have a drink!" He explains: "Anyone who believes in me will have rivers of living water flowing out of their heart, just like the Bible says!" (7:37–38).

The biblical reference here, most would agree, is the closing section of the prophecy of Ezekiel (47:1–12). There, following a long description of the rebuilding of the Temple after the Exile, the prophet describes the river of the water of life flowing out of the Temple and down to the Dead Sea, making it fresh. It looks as though Jesus is here promising that his followers, those who believe in him and come to him to quench their thirst, will themselves become life carriers, able to quench the thirst of others. That is certainly what is in mind in 20:21, when Jesus breathes the Spirit on his followers and commissions them to be for the world what he had been for Israel.

John explains this further in 7:39. Jesus was, he says, talking about the Spirit, which believers would receive. "The spirit wasn't available yet," he says, "because Jesus was not yet glorified." This too is Temple-related. The glorious divine Presence cannot enter a polluted shrine. The foot-washing scene indicates what is going on: the disciples are already "made clean" by the word Jesus has spoken to them (13:10; 15:3), but Jesus's coming crucifixion, symbolized by the foot washing, will cleanse them completely. And this cleansing, as with the sacrificial cult in Israel's Temple, is not (as it were) for their own sake or so that they can then leave this world and go to be with God. It is the other way around. They are "cleansed" so that the glorious divine Presence, God's own very self in the person of the Spirit, can come and dwell with them and in them.

These complex and challenging sayings seem clearly to be pointing to something that has already happened during Jesus's public career as he has spoken God's word to his followers. There are two conversations, early in the gospel narrative, where we can see something like this happening. In both, Jesus's promise about the Spirit is central.

The first is the conversation in chapter 3 with Nicodemus, Jesus's nocturnal visitor. The fact that he comes at night is the sort of thing John likes to stress. For him, "darkness" and "light" are symbolic, as we see graphically when Judas leaves the Last Supper and "it was night" (13:30). So John draws attention to the nighttime visit here, presumably indicating that Nicodemus is typical of those who have not yet come to faith.

Nicodemus's opening line, a kind of challenge ("Is Jesus really a teacher from God, and if so what exactly is he trying to do?") is met with what looks like a non sequitur—something that happens a lot in John. "Let's cut through the preliminary courtesies," Jesus seems to be saying, "and get to the point. God's kingdom is coming, the new day for which Israel had longed. But don't imagine that simply being a senior member of the Judaean establishment will be enough to make you part of that new world." There is another requirement:

> Let me tell you the solemn truth. Unless someone has
> been born from above, they won't be able to see God's
> kingdom. (3:3)

The term translated "from above" can also mean "anew" or "again." But since Jesus goes on to talk about the fact that his "birth" comes from God rather than from human origin (rather like what is said in the prologue in 1:12–13, and what is said about the kingdom itself in 18:36), it looks as though the primary meaning here is indeed "from above." Nicodemus objects to this. (This again is typical of conversations in John: people regularly misunderstand what Jesus says, and Jesus then has to put them right.) What on earth, says the learned teacher, can you mean by speaking of a second birth?

Jesus's answer draws together echoes of the baptism that John the Baptist had begun, which Jesus himself continued to practice with his followers (3:22). This baptism seems to have been a way of recruiting kingdom workers, "new Exodus" people, water-and-Spirit people, people longing for God's new day to dawn, people who were hoping and praying that the movement that had begun with John the Baptist and was now continuing with Jesus would be the catalyst. Thus:

> "I'm telling you the solemn truth," replied Jesus. "Unless someone is born from water and spirit, they can't enter God's kingdom. Flesh is born from flesh, but spirit is born from spirit. Don't be surprised that I said to you, You must be born from above. The wind blows where it wants to, and you hear the sound it makes; but you don't know where it's coming from or where it's going to. That's what it's like with someone who is born from the spirit." (3:5–8)

Here we are at the heart of the rich spirituality in which the living, powerful presence of God, like the pillar of cloud and fire at the Exodus, leads the people through the water and then comes to dwell right in their midst—only now not in a tent, but through the Spirit in the very interior of each and every believer. New creation is going ahead, doing surprising things, not sticking to old boundary markers.

God is thus calling out a new family, and though the members of the old family (Abraham's physical descendants) are of course eagerly invited to belong, there is no guarantee they will avail themselves of this. Every Jewish renewal movement of the period thought like this: when God did the new thing he had promised, you had to get on board or you would miss out. John had already said as much in the prologue: "his own people" didn't receive Jesus, but anyone and everyone who did so gained the right to Israel's title, "children of God." And "they were not born from blood, or from fleshly desire, or from the intention of a man, but from God" (1:13). This offers the ultimate response to the puzzled spirituality questions of our day: a personal heaven-and-earth link, a new genuinely human "identity" of the highest order, a gift from the Creator himself.

The other conversation that makes the same point comes in John 4. This is Jesus's lighthearted but deadly serious conversation with the Samaritan woman. Again, the topic of Israel's inheritance and the Temple is to the fore, and again Jesus slices through the questions with the promise of a new worship, a new spirituality, a new intimacy.

The conversation moves forward to the point at which Jesus puts his finger on the real sorrow and muddle in the woman's personal life. As often occurs at such a moment, the person who feels put on the spot abruptly changes tack, often to some item of "religious" controversy, thinking that that should steer the conversation away from the awkward personal challenge! So, faced with the question about her marital life, the woman quickly asks Jesus about the clash of Temples. Her ancestors, she says, worshipped on a mountain in Samaria (Gerizim), and the Jews say worship should be in Jerusalem.

Any good Jew would of course know the standard answer

to that: Jerusalem was indeed the place where Israel's God, the world's creator, had decided to place his name, his gracious presence. But Jesus sees Jerusalem as simply a pointer to the new reality he has come to put into effect:

> "Believe me, woman," replied Jesus, "the time is coming when you won't worship the father on this mountain or in Jerusalem. . . . The time is coming—indeed, it's here already!—when true worshippers will worship the father in spirit and in truth. Yes: that's the kind of worshippers the father is looking for. God is spirit, and those who worship him must worship in spirit and in truth."
> (4:21–24).

This conversation must be seen alongside the nighttime consultation with Nicodemus. The learned Jewish teacher must discover that being born a Jew isn't enough. Something new needs to happen, something that will fulfill scripture in a whole new way, something that will launch the new Exodus, the new covenant, with the divine Presence coming to dwell right inside God's people, as Jeremiah (31) and Ezekiel (36) had always promised. And the Samaritan woman needs to look beyond not only her messed-up personal life but also the age-old rivalry between Jew and Samaritan. God is doing a new thing, and "worship" will be a matter of Spirit and reality.

The promised Spirit, then, is the dynamic of Johannine spirituality. This answers today's contemporary questions with an enormous sigh of relief. Whatever has happened in the past, the life-transforming work of God's Spirit can make all things new.

There is much more we could say, and we will circle back

to this topic from time to time in what follows. But here is the contribution John makes to our contemporary discussion about spirituality. Forget "religion" in the old sense or in the muddled ways people still use that word today. Forget the confused rebellions and counterrebellions of the 1960s and all the other periods and movements that have shaped today's Western culture. Learn to think with the mind of a Second Temple Jew, believing that heaven and earth were designed to overlap; discovering that the Temple, where that happened supremely, was itself being replaced by this young man called Jesus; and discovering too that the Torah, the divine law that refreshed and enlivened your innermost thoughts, feelings, motives, and emotions, was now upstaged by God's own Spirit, freely offered, enabling you to worship from the heart and to serve God in a whole new way.

"The law was given through Moses," John wrote toward the end of the prologue; "grace and truth came through Jesus the Messiah" (1:17). That is the recipe for a genuine, transformative, Jesus-focused spirituality, which will upstage the self-serving and often narcissistic parodies on offer in many quarters today.

With this, we reach the same point that we got to with the signposts justice and love. What Jesus offers in the gospel is the true, refreshing water of life. Those who taste it know that whatever they have been using up to now to quench their thirst, including the gnostic tendency to seek answers inside themselves, is at best not working and at worst poisonous. But the living water confirms that the thirst was a true signpost to the reality. The presence of Jesus and the power of the Spirit confirm that to be human was and is a good thing; being creatures of space, time, and matter was and is good; and that the powerful, rescuing, healing, transforming love of God is renewing the whole world, and ourselves with it. That is the meaning of Johannine spirituality. And that points forward to our next broken signpost: we live in a beautiful world, but ugliness often seems to have the last word.

The Messiah in John

A major theme in John's picture of Jesus is messiahship. There was no single model of messiahship in the Jewish world at the time. Various scriptural sources all contributed to the prevailing idea of a warrior king who would get rid of Israel's enemies, build or restore the Temple so that God would come and live there again, and bring peace and justice to the world. That's why many people were puzzled when Jesus seemed to be doing and saying striking things, but still didn't fit the idea of "messiah" they might have held (e.g., 7:31–52).

But John, like Paul, sees a clue. In two or three passages in the scriptures, the coming king is spoken of as the "son of God." That is clear in 2 Samuel 7:12–14; Psalm 2:7; and 89:26–27. These famous biblical passages were well known in Jesus's day. But, so far as we can tell, nobody then was linking them to the idea that, if and when the messiah turned up, he would somehow *embody* Israel's God in person in a way for which the language of "father and son" would be the most appropriate expression.

Throughout the early Christian movement, however, this conclusion was being drawn. The early disciples quickly realized that it matched up with the vivid way in which Jesus had spoken of "my father" or "the father who sent me." We see it in Paul and especially here in John. A full study would take a whole book, but we may just look at two passages, one early on in the fourth gospel and one near the end.

At the end of chapter 1 Jesus has a strange conversation with a new disciple, Nathanael, who is initially very suspicious. After a bit of banter ("Wait a minute. Are you telling me that you believe just because I told you I saw you under the fig tree?" 1:50), there comes one of the "solemn truth" moments: "You'll see heaven opened, and God's angels ascending and descending on the son of man" (1:51). This strange, complex saying comes to life when we realize that Jesus is alluding to the story of Jacob. In Jacob's dream there was a ladder set up between heaven and earth. That idea, in the ancient world, would remind people of a Tabernacle or Temple, a place where heaven and earth were joined (see Gen. 28:10–22). But what Jesus is saying here is that the "ladder" is now *Jesus himself*, seen as the "son of man."

That too is confusing. The phrase "son of man" could, in Jesus's day, simply mean "I" or "someone like me." But its use elsewhere in the gospels, and particularly in John, points us to Daniel 7. There, "one like a son of man," representing God's true people, is exalted after apparent suffering and ends up sitting on a throne next to the "Ancient of Days."

Jesus's comment to Nathanael may still seem oblique, dense to the point of incomprehension. But when we read the exchange between Jesus and Nathanael in the light of the whole book, it begins to make sense. Nathanael had questioned whether Jesus could really be the messiah. Jesus is saying that this will become clear, but that messiahship itself is to be seen as a vocation to join heaven and earth together, to do and be for Israel and the world what the Temple was and did. This is then immediately confirmed in the next chapter, where John explains that Jesus was "speaking of the 'temple' of his body."

The same point emerges, in very different ways, in the closing passages of the book—that is, in the original ending, since we assume that chapter 21 was added sometime later. Thomas famously declares that he won't believe that Jesus is risen unless he can touch and see the marks made by the nails and the spear. Jesus—with a smile, we must assume!—invites Thomas to do just that: to touch and see. Fascinatingly, John does not say that Thomas actually did reach out and touch the wounds. Instead, he has Thomas say, "My Lord and my God!" (20:28).

This is the first time in the whole book that someone has used the word "God" to address Jesus. John is bringing us back to where he started, with the Word who was and is God. Now, he is saying, all is revealed. And then comes the "official" conclusion:

> Jesus did many other signs in the presence of his disciples, which aren't written in this book. But these are written so that you may believe that the Messiah, the son of God, is none other than Jesus; and that, with this faith, you may have life in his name. (20:30–31)

People debate whether the "you" here refers to people who have not yet believed or people who have believed but need to go on doing so. That doesn't matter so much for our discussion. What matters is the precise focus of that last sentence.

Most translations put it like this: "that you may believe that Jesus is the Messiah [Christ], the son of God." In other words,

John would be saying, "You've heard of Jesus. Now I've shown you that he is the Messiah, the son of God." But the Greek strongly suggests that it is the other way around. Like Andrew, Peter, Philip, and Nathanael in 1:35–51, there is already a question in the air about a messiah who will be the "son of God" in the "royal" sense of Psalm 2. But now John has shown that this "Messiah, son of God" is *none other than Jesus himself.* That was what the book was designed to demonstrate.

This means that in John, as in Paul, we are watching the phrase "son of God" do something that hadn't been done before—because nobody had thought it needed to be attempted. This powerful little phrase now holds together two meanings that had originally been distinct. In Jewish writing, "son of God" could be used for Israel (e.g., Hos. 11:1) or, as we saw, for the messiah. Sometimes, indeed, it could also be used to designate angelic beings (e.g., Gen. 6:4; Job 1:6). But the earliest followers of Jesus seem to have realized that with Jesus himself, who constantly referred to his "father" and even suggested that he and the Father were "one" (John 10:30) and that anyone who had seen him had seen the Father (14:9), the phrase "son of God" was the natural and appropriate way of holding together the two previously unconnected strands.

There was, on the one hand, the idea of Israel's messiah. There was, on the other, the altogether larger and more mind-boggling notion that Israel's God, in fulfillment of his ancient promises, would come to dwell as a human being among his people and would there overcome the dark forces of evil, rescue Israel and the world from their grip, and launch the new creation. In other words, just as John is suggesting by his placing of 1:14 ("the Word became flesh") that there is an utter *appropriateness* about the In-

carnation, so he is suggesting throughout his gospel that there is
an utter appropriateness about Israel's messiah being this "tabernacling" presence of God.

To be sure, we cannot fit all these notions together as though
they were part of a mathematical equation or an experiment in
high-energy physics. But within the narrative and prophecies
of Israel's scriptures, John insists, it makes every possible sense.
When we look at Jesus and recognize him to be Israel's messiah,
we also realize that in this Messiah the living God, the God of
Abraham, Isaac, and Jacob, the I AM who rescued Israel from
Egypt, has at last fulfilled his greatest promise to come and dwell
with his people. He has come in person, in the person of the
long-awaited Messiah, to rescue them and to bring about his
new creation.

Chapter Four

Beauty

THE MOON HAS ONLY A FEW DAYS LEFT IN ITS CYCLE, rising now in the southeast about two hours before dawn. I stood outside this morning in the frosty air, under a totally clear sky, marveling one more time at the infinite number of twinkling lights above me, small messages sent out so long ago that it makes the events in John's gospel seem like yesterday. There was the moon, low and dramatic in its late crescent. To its left was the planet Venus, bright as the light of a landing plane; and there, to its right, was Jupiter, not so bright but with its own glowing beauty. I had to come indoors, but returned several more times, and as the sun came up three or four flocks of geese rose with it, honking and flapping on their morning journey, flying right past the bright crescent and the still visible planets.

It is cloudy now. The geese have gone, and so has the glory

of the night. I am enriched and also saddened. Such astonishing beauty, so soon over. Yes, it will return, though as always there is the sense of longing, of hope that this time, this time, it will last. C. S. Lewis once wrote a poem about the false promise of spring, with the birds singing that this time summer will go on forever.

Of course I know that if the moon and the planets were just hanging in the sky in exactly the same place day after day, even they would lose their charm. Just as I know that if my grand-daughter never grew up, but lived in a perpetual Peter Pan–like childhood, always with that same heart-melting smile and impetuous affection, I would know (as would others) that something was very wrong. And my favorite moments in my favorite music are what they are precisely because they come just *then*, they say *that* to me (though they say it in different ways every time I hear it), and then they are a memory, absorbed first into the onward flow of the music and then into my expanded heart. I was going to say, they become "just" a memory, but perhaps that's wrong too. They are part of who I am.

But even that is a puzzle. I too am as transient as the moon, as the geese, as the symphony. Having reached what the Psalmist saw as my natural allotted time, the beauty-formed person I have become (and, yes, the person also made ugly by folly and sin) will be turned back to the dust from which I came. Was it for this, asked World War I poet Wilfred Owen, that the clay grew tall?

We are all of us hardwired for beauty, searching for a deeper and richer meaning in a world that sometimes seems to overflow with delight but at other times feels dreadful and cold. Beauty— the haunting sense of loveliness, the transient yet utterly powerful stabs of something like love but something more and different as well—is not after all a mere evolutionary twist, an echo of an atavistic urge to hunt prey, to find a mate, or to escape danger. It is a pointer to the strange, gently demanding presence of the living God in the midst of his world.

But, as death itself discloses, if beauty is in some ways a signpost to a deeper reality, to the truth of God himself, it is nevertheless a broken signpost. Our poisoned world falls so far short of the aesthetic or the sacred ideal. Perhaps that is why art has become such a challenge. The last generation of young British artists has been notorious for its portrayal of ugliness, of life's sordid realities, inviting us to see, in the words of playwright Harold Pinter, "the weasel under the cocktail cabinet." The whole movement is sneering at the pretensions of today's world. In reacting against sentimentalism, against dreamy fantasy, our culture has swung around to embrace brutalism, whose concrete-tower blocks trample on our romantic visions of fairy castles and cozy cottages. This infects our political life too, torn as it so often is between those who want to return to a fantasy of "how things were in better times" and those who insist that those "better times" were oppressive and hollow. We have been shown the seamy side of life so often that our cultural clothes now appear to be nothing but seams.

There is a nihilism about this prevailing mood, a kind of death worship that goes much farther than the in-love-with-death theme of the nineteenth-century Romantics. Philosopher Theodore Adorno said that one cannot write poetry after Auschwitz. I think this is what he meant: that beauty, like justice, has disappeared from the world, so we must not try to make things better. Auschwitz, after all, is where they say that no birds sing to this day. Perhaps the human songbirds must also fall silent before the total ugliness and (as political philosopher Hannah Arendt commented) the sheer banality of evil, on public display right there at the heart of the supposedly civilized world.

But perhaps there are yet ways. Benjamin Britten's *War Requiem*, setting poems by Wilfred Owen, was trying at least to make a dark and solemn beauty out of it all, just as the second movement of Beethoven's First String Quartet (op. 18, no. 1) was a deliberate attempt to evoke the tragic finale of *Romeo and Juliet*. Perhaps part of the role of beauty is actually to help us find grace within grief. Perhaps.

Yet into this brokenness comes a God who seems to care deeply about beauty, a God who, according to the Bible, created the heavens and the earth to tell of his glory—not because he needed us to admire that glory, but because the glory was a true outflowing of his own generous love. What's more, this God dares to whisper to us, even in the midst of our fractured world, that we are created in his own image and that this God-reflecting vocation can be and is being restored. This is in fact a major theme of the New Testament. But how does that work out? How can we make sense of it all? How can beauty be anything other than a broken signpost?

A Glorious God

At first glance the Bible doesn't seem to say much about beauty. If you look up "beauty" in a concordance, you won't find many references, though there are some, and they are important. And I fear that some of what the Bible *does* say about beauty, though not necessarily using that word, has been screened out by the rather severe traditions of reading and studying scripture that have gone looking for dogma rather than delight. If you spend your time asking whether the second half of the book of Exodus came from a fourth-century source rather than a tenth-century one and worrying about which bits of text were imported by a later redactor, you may be focusing on the wrong thing. You would be like someone going into a wonderful art gallery and concentrating on the different types of picture frames.

But the second half of the book of Exodus is, from one point of view, all about beauty. It is about the commissioning and construction of the wilderness Tabernacle, whose vivid colors and rich decoration must have been all the more striking in the midst of a barren desert. And it is to the Tabernacle that John's gospel directs our attention right from the start. The Word became flesh, he says, and *tabernacled* in our midst.

John's gospel, of course, is not theory. It is narrative. It is narrative in the great Hebrew tradition, drawing explicitly on the themes and strands in Genesis and Exodus, in the Psalms and Isaiah. The "Word" who becomes "flesh" can mean many things, but was undoubtedly heard by some educated readers in the ancient world in terms of the *logos* idea in ancient Stoicism and Platonism. But the larger context in John 1 and thereafter insists that the primary meaning comes from the Hebrew scriptures. It is the Word by which the heavens were made (Ps. 33:6), the creative Word that will endure forever though all "flesh" may perish (Isa. 40:6–8), the Word that will go out like rain or snow and accomplish God's work in the world, specif-ically the new creation that will arise after the catastrophes of the old (55:10–11).

John's haunting prologue, evoking these contexts and many others, itself touches the poetic heights, bringing together the story of the Creator and his world with the human story of John the Baptist and Jesus, the human challenge to believe and be-come one of God's children, and the utterly human, image-bearing, glory-filled story of the "Word made flesh." There are many things that are better said in poetry than in prose. John's prologue is a kind of exalted, quasi-poetic prose, and it pulls together many strands of meaning and beauty. The prologue thus functions like a great doorway, inviting us into a house that is itself filled, corridor by corridor, room by room, with more beauty.

If the beauty of creation is a constant pointer to the "glory of God," and if the story of Jesus is the story of his unveiling of that "glory," then we ought to be reading this story with our eyes and ears open for that kind of meaning. And here, to be sure, it is. The vivid and haunting exchanges between Jesus and his friends, Jesus and his mother, and Jesus and strangers; Jesus's unexpected actions and flights of explanation—all this suffuses the down-to-earth first-century story with beauty, in the way that twilight invests ordinary objects and scenes with a sudden strange meaning.

The quality of John's writing achieves this aim. Jesus "dis-played his glory," he says, summing up the first "sign" (2:11). Jesus went on doing so, opening the eyes of those nearby—or of some of them at least. John's telling of the story, at the next level, opens the eyes of his readers to see the beauty of creation transformed by the personal presence of the creative Word.

John, then, is drawing upon a rich biblical history when he speaks of the unveiling of God's glory. "Strength and beauty are in his sanctuary," sings the Psalmist (96:6), using the same word (*tiphereth*) as in Exodus 28:2 and 28:40, when God commands Moses to make the richly adorned vestments for Aaron and his sons, literally, "for glory and for beauty" (we will come back to this presently). This Hebrew word is rare. Sometimes in its other uses it overlaps with meanings for which we might say "honor," "pomp," or "majesty." The ancient Hebrews, in other words, did not isolate the idea of "beauty" the way modern Westerners have often done. It was woven in with other themes as well, including the most important, "glory."

As we noticed in the last chapter, the idea of divine glory coming to dwell in the Tabernacle and then in the Temple in Jerusalem was part of the larger theological vision of the Hebrew scriptures. The hints we get from various passages suggest that the glorious divine Presence within these consecrated structures was itself a thing of what we would call great beauty. It inspired awe, devotion, love, and worship in the way that a hulking stone pyramid might never do.

As we all know, when you meet something, or indeed someone, really beautiful, you don't need to be *told* to admire it; you are "filled with admiration," as we say, by the sight or sound of it. That's what's happening, I think, in another psalm where the poet declares that God makes the mornings and evenings to praise him (65:8). The enhanced sunlight, refracted through the atmosphere, lends to the earliest and the latest moments of the day a strange, evocative quality that noon does not need.

These ideas could, indeed, be the basis of what some call "natural theology"—the possibility that by contemplating things in the present world we might deduce eternal truths about God. One might read Psalm 19 in that light, and indeed I was thinking of Psalm 19 as I gazed at the moon with (so it seemed) its two escorting planets just before sunrise this morning:

> The heavens are telling the glory of God;
> And the firmament proclaims his handiwork.
> Day to day pours forth speech, and night to night
> declares knowledge.
> There is no speech, nor are there words; their voice
> is not heard;
> Yet their voice goes out through all the earth, and their
> words to the end of the world. (19:1–4)

"Glory" in that first line is *kabod*, the normal Hebrew word that serves as a catchall for the weighty and awesome, but also stunningly beautiful, presence of God. It then comes to refer to anything and everything that reflects or embodies that strange, powerful, hard-to-pin-down sense of something more, something greater, something more intimate than what you would get from a chemical or mathematical analysis.

And here in the midst of it all is God-in-Jesus, the Word made flesh, calmly unveiling God's glory, the glory of new creation, the glory promised in the previously not quite understood scriptures, and inviting belief. *The Word became flesh and lived among us, and we gazed upon his glory.* If we stop still for a moment and hold our breath, we might just glimpse it.

In the Image of God

Putting the larger biblical story together, we find several hints suggesting that one of the reasons we yearn for beauty is that we are created in the very image of God. The idea of the "image" has to do with *reflection*: humans have the vocation of reflecting the power and glory of the Creator into the world. In this, the biblical message is radically different from the ideas prevalent in the cultures surrounding the Israelites.

Think, again, of the pyramids. The enslaved Israelites knew the great pyramids in Egypt, of which the biggest, already over a thousand years old by the time of Moses, remains the single largest construction in the world. They are, as we saw in an earlier chapter, quite massive. But they are impersonal, dehumanizing, monstrous, declaring to all and sundry something of the sheer power of the kings for whose burial they were designed and of the gods that were worshipped in that culture.

Then consider the description of the Tabernacle in Exodus 25–30 and its actual manufacture—after the terrible rebellion centered around the golden calf—in chapters 35–39. Notable within both passages is the fact that, along with the construction of the Tabernacle itself, there are detailed instructions for the making of robes and other ornaments for the priests, and specially for Aaron and his sons. Our anti-hierarchical age may instinctively rebel against such exaltation of one family, but that misses the point. In this construction, instead of a dead king, as with the pyramids, there is a live priest. The God who is to be worshipped here is the God in whose image humans were made. The rich robes worn by the priest are a sign that this God wants to raise up human beings from their dusty desert existence and make them "a kingdom of priests and a holy nation" (Exod. 19:6, RSV).

We shouldn't be surprised, then, to find that instead of massive blocks of stone brought by thousands of slaves (archaeologists have variously calculated the thousands of people and the length of time it took to build those pyramids), Moses is commanded in Exodus 25 to collect materials for great, colorful, sparkling beauty:

> Gold, silver, and bronze, blue, purple, and crimson yarns and fine linen, goats' hair, tanned rams' skins, fine leather, acacia wood, oil for the lamps, spices for the anointing oil and for the fragrant incense, onyx stones and gems to be set in the ephod and for the breastpiece. (25:3–7)

The building, its furnishings, and the priests' vestments are lavishly described and then, after the unfortunate hiatus around the golden calf, lavishly created. At no point does the text say, "Look how beautiful all this is"—except perhaps in those passages we just noted where Aaron's vestments are described as being "for glory and for beauty." But that is part of the point. Only a poor writer says, "It was exciting," "It was beautiful," or "It was terrifying." A good writer (and John is certainly a good writer) makes you *feel* and *imagine* the beauty and excitement without spelling it out.

But if we read the second half of Exodus straight through, thinking of the slave people who have left the land of the pyramids and are now in the wild and desolate Sinai Peninsula and are about to make something of extraordinary and life-enhancing beauty—we are bound to see this as an amazing and celebratory accomplishment. The Tabernacle was meant to delight the eye, the nose, the ear, and not least the imagination. And part of the point was that it was to be a work of great art and skill. Those involved in the construction and decoration were themselves being ennobled by being involved in God's planned beauty, God's intended dwelling, this "little cosmos," this heaven-and-earth building they had been instructed to make.

And this is just the start. It is all preparation, again not for a dead king and his potential postmortem existence in some imagined underworld, but for the living God, the powerful and glorious Creator of all, who would come and fill this Tabernacle with his presence. This is a God who delights in beauty and wants his image-bearing human creatures to make more and more of it.

This theme is picked up in another key psalm, Psalm 8. There, musing on the mystery of human life amid the vast cosmos, the poet declares that, though humans are indeed below the level of the angels, they are "crowned with glory and honor" (*kabod* and *hadar*). The basis for this role is the dominion over God's world given them in Genesis 1, reflecting their image-bearing vocation.

The fact that humans are created in God's image points toward the overall way in which God's sublime presence permeates the "ordinary" world throughout John's gospel. We see this clearly in the wonderful and evocative Good Shepherd discourse in 10:1–18. You don't have to work on a farm to sense the beauty of the image, developing as it does Isaiah's picture of God coming to "feed his flock like a shepherd, . . . gather the lambs in his arms, . . . and gently lead the mother sheep" (40:11). (It also parallels the prophecy of the shepherd king in Ezek. 34 and the much darker shepherd picture in Zech. 11:11–17; 13:7.) Though this discourse too is fraught with danger—Jesus is constantly contrasting himself with rival claimants to kingship—it is full of poetic power:

> "I'm telling you the solemn truth," said Jesus. "Anyone who doesn't come into the sheepfold by the gate, but gets in by some other way, is a thief and a brigand. But the one who comes in through the gate is the sheep's own shepherd. The doorkeeper will open up for him, and the sheep hear his voice. He calls his own sheep by name, and leads them out. When he has brought out all that belong to him, he goes on ahead of them. The sheep follow him, because they know his voice. They won't follow a stranger; instead, they will run away from him, because they don't know the stranger's voice. . . .
>
> "I am the gate. If anyone comes in by me, they will be safe, and will go in and out and find pasture. The thief only comes to steal, and kill, and destroy. I came so that they could have life—yes, and have it full to overflowing." (10:1–5, 9–10)

This passage is a beautiful expression of a picture that is itself beautiful, describing a reality that is more beautiful yet.

And that reality, for those with ears to hear (especially with their ears attuned to John's scriptural heritage), is the suffusing of the ordinary—a real human being navigating his vocation against real opposition, with the fate of real people hanging on his words—with the extraordinary, or rather with the divine.

In Ezekiel 34, this sense of the divine Presence suffusing the human reality comes through when we try to figure out just who is the "shepherd" who will come and sort everything out. Will it be God himself, as it seems to begin with, or will it be David, the coming king, as it seems later on? I think the prophet is saying, "Both, actually," though without explaining how.

And it is in that overlap, that sudden realization that *truly* YHWH *is in this place*, as Jacob said when he awoke from his dream of the ladder between heaven and earth (Gen. 28:16), that we sense the presence of the sublime: something "more" is, as we say, "going on." (The fact that we resort to arm-waving language at that point is an indication both that something needs to be said and that we quickly run out of appropriate words to say it.) To put it in somewhat grandiose language, the enveloping sense of the transcendent in the commonplace points to the living, loving, mysterious, and joyful Creator, who made us in his image, a little lower than the angels, in order to call us and enable us to reflect his loving creativity into his world.

Resurrection Beauty

John's preoccupation with beauty comes to the fore in the magnificent scene in John 11 in which Jesus raises Lazarus. Someone should really make it into an opera; it has all the required qualities. The beauty of the story as a whole, I think, lies in the way the climax—Lazarus coming alive out of the tomb—is framed, end to end, with the smell of death, of which Martha was afraid when Jesus told them to take away the stone from the mouth of the tomb. In the opening paragraph (11:1–16) a message comes to Jesus that Lazarus is deathly ill—but Jesus decides to stay where he is for two days. Why doesn't he go? Perhaps, think the disciples, because Bethany is near Jerusalem, and the Judaeans (those who live in Jerusalem and its vicinity) had been plotting to kill him. Jesus doesn't deny this. Indeed, the idea of Jesus's own death, as well as Lazarus's, is important as part of the frame of the story. Thomas, gloomy as ever, sums it up. If they must go to Jerusalem, they must go. "Let's go too," he says. "We may as well die with him" (11:16). The scene is set.

But the central action of the story is all about new life. Martha and Mary rebuke Jesus for not coming sooner. The dialogue is swift, sharp, and poignant; if we really get inside it, it won't only be Jesus who is near to tears as we approach the climax. Then comes the moment, suffused with that special light that made the Psalmist sing:

> "Take away the stone," said Jesus.
> "But, Master," said Martha, the dead man's sister, "there'll be a smell! It's the fourth day already!"
> "Didn't I tell you," said Jesus, "that if you believed you would see God's glory?"
> So they took the stone away. (11:39–41)

Now at this point John's alert readers want to know: "So, was there a smell? If not, why not?" John gives us the answer by telling us, instead, what Jesus did next. He prayed a prayer—not of petition ("Please, will you give Lazarus back his life"), but of *thanksgiving*. Something had happened when they took the stone away—which meant he already knew the answer to the prayer he had prayed earlier, prayed in those two dark days when the smell of death was upon them:

> "Thank you, Father," he said, "for hearing me! I know you always hear me, but I've said this because of the crowd standing around, so that they may believe that you sent me." (11:41–42)

Now all that remained was to make public and visible what was already achieved:

> With these words, he gave a loud shout: "Lazarus—come out!" (11:43)

Perhaps it shouldn't be an opera. Perhaps a play or a movie. Imagine a pause. Everyone holds their breath. Then—

> And the dead man came out. He was tied up, hand and foot, with strips of linen, and his face was wrapped in a cloth.
> "Untie him," said Jesus, "and let him go." (11:44)

New life has burst out in the middle of a world of death. But a world of death is what it still is. Some of the bystanders went off to tell Jesus's critics what had happened. The chief priests met to decide, in advance of any trial, that Jesus himself would have to die. The beauty of the entire scene is that the powerful promise of life bursts into a world still framed by death. In John's literary artistry, that functions as a picture of what the whole gospel is doing.

All of this leads, as John intends it to do, to Jesus's own death, the place where the divine glory is fully and finally revealed. Except that it isn't final, because with Jesus's own resurrection (carefully distinguished from that of Lazarus, in that Lazarus comes out still bound in the grave cloths, whereas Jesus, mysteriously, leaves his grave cloths behind in 20:6–7) we have a new beginning. Here too John's description does what the world's greatest paintings do: it invites us to stand in silence and contemplate beauty beyond words:

> On the first day of the week, very early, Mary Magdalene came to the tomb while it was still dark. She saw that the stone had been rolled away from the tomb. So she ran off, and went to Simon Peter, and to the other disciple, the one Jesus loved.
>
> "They've taken the master out of the tomb!" she said. "We don't know where they've put him!"
>
> So Peter and the other disciple set off and went to the tomb. Both of them ran together. The other disciple ran faster than Peter, and got to the tomb first. He stooped down and saw the linen cloths lying there, but he didn't go in. Then Simon Peter came up, following him, and went into the tomb. He saw the linen cloths lying there, and the napkin that had been around his head, not lying with the other cloths, but folded up in a place by itself.
>
> Then the other disciple, who had arrived first at

the tomb, went into the tomb as well. He saw, and he
believed. They did not yet know, you see, that the Bible
had said he must rise again from the dead.

Then the disciples returned to their homes. (20:1–10)

Part of the artistry here, I think, is that in spite of a very busy
scene—people running to and fro in the half-light—we sense all
the way through that behind this busy-ness, this panicky dash-
ing about, there is a great, glad, calm reality being unveiled, so
joyful that it is also solemn and serious, so vast as to be beyond
telling. *Yes*, we think, *isn't that how it always is?* All we humans
seem to be able to do is to blunder about in the dark, trying to
get it right, not quite understanding. And then, just when we
think it is all nonsense, God does something huge and powerful.
And, yes, beautiful.

John's resurrection account thus evokes an intangible sense of
the Word made flesh, of the holy in the midst of our world, of
beauty emerging from the thing that most obviously challenges
it, the horrible corruption of death itself. It isn't surprising that
Mary and the others can't yet grasp it. But as we saw earlier
when we explored John's connection between the Temple and
Jesus's incarnation, his story of the resurrection stands in a strong
biblical tradition that sheds a powerful light on the way in which
the true God desires to dwell among us.

In John's prologue, remember, the Word became flesh and
tabernacled in our midst. That is the point to which John now
returns. In the wilderness Tent, the very center, the holiest spot
of all, was in the innermost part, the Holy of Holies. And there,
instead of an "image" of God, was the "covenant box," the ark
of the covenant, a chest containing the tablets of the Torah. The

lid of the ark was the "mercy seat," the place where God had promised to come, to meet with his people. This was the space that, once a year on the Day of Atonement, the high priest entered to be in the presence of Israel's covenant God. This is what John now appears to have in mind.

At either end of the mercy seat, carved gloriously out of the same gold as the covering itself, were two cherubs (Exod. 37:6–9). If the Tabernacle as a whole was the great symbol of beauty, the beauty of creation and new creation, even in a barren world and among a rebellious people, this piece of furniture was the sign that when God wanted to meet with his people, this too would be a moment of radiant beauty. Now John takes that image—the angels at either end of the mercy seat, the place where God would meet his people in beauty and grace—and tells us that now Israel's God has, in Jesus, met with his people once and for all. He has set up his Tabernacle once and for all and has launched the new creation for which the wonderful Tabernacle itself was simply an advance sign:

> But Mary stood outside the tomb, crying. As she wept, she stooped down to look into the tomb. There she saw two angels, clothed in white, one at the head and one at the feet of where Jesus's body had been lying. (20:11–12)

The angels ask Mary why she is crying, and she explains. But John's explanation is already there, hiding in plain sight. Mary embodies the sorrow of Israel, the long lament that stretches back to the griefs of the Israelite women at the slaughter of their children in Egypt, the despair of the exiles in Babylon, the unhealed hurts that burst out in the Psalms, the tragic suffering that sobs its way, line by line, through the Lamentations of Jeremiah. Why, they ask, is she crying? Well, why would she not be crying? Why would the world not be crying? And, with the answer, John's writing embodies the inner secret of beauty itself, the beauty that refuses to be trivialized into sentimentalism or rejected in the pseudo-realist brutalism that laughs bitterly at the thought that there had ever been such a thing as hope:

> "They've taken away my master," she said, "and I don't know where they've put him!"
>
> As she said this she turned around and saw Jesus standing there. She didn't know it was Jesus.
>
> "Woman," Jesus said to her, "why are you crying? Who are you looking for?"
>
> She guessed he must be the gardener.
>
> "Sir," she said, "if you've carried him off somewhere, tell me where you've put him, and I will take him away."
>
> "Mary!" said Jesus.
>
> She turned and spoke in Aramaic.
>
> "Rabbouni!" she said (which means "Teacher").
>
> "Don't cling to me," said Jesus. "I haven't yet gone up to the father. But go to my brothers and say to them, 'I'm going up to my father and your father—to my God and your God.'"
>
> Mary Magdalene went and told the disciples, "I've seen the master!" and that he had said these things to her. (20:13–18)

With this double scene—the two disciples in vv. 1–10, and Mary in vv. 11–18—John has brought his larger picture full circle. It needs completing in the rest of the chapter, and we shall return to that, but already we can see what has happened. *This is all about new creation.* It is the "first day of the week"; not all translations put those as the first words of the chapter, but that's how John wrote it. And he repeats them when describing the evening in v. 19. The work of the previous "week" has been completed, and now new creation can and will begin.

There are echoes of the prologue—the early light, the new life, the invitation to be "children of God," and above all the "tabernacling" presence of the incarnate Son. And, with that, there are the strong echoes of Genesis. In the scene of Jesus and Mary in the garden, this "daughter of Eve" is supposing that this "son of Adam" is the gardener, as indeed he is. He is now making all things new. He is doing so in himself, as the first fruits of new creation. Through his new authority, he is bringing new creation to life all around him.

With that, our own argument in this chapter comes full circle. Our human drive for beauty, for transcendent meaning, turns out to be more than we ever expected. It is God-given: a signpost, designed to lead us back to his presence. Ah, we sigh, but it ends in darkness and horror, with the dust of death covering over the beauty in thick, choking layers of ugliness. Yes, says John, but see what the creator God now does. He makes a way through death and out the other side into new creation, new beauty, new life.

In both the substance of this story and the manner of its telling, John is speaking of a beauty that had always been pointing back to its maker, even though "the world was made through him, and the world did not know him" (1:10). By focusing our attention, in his telling of Jesus's story, on the Tabernacle and Temple as well as the world of creation, John was picking up their ultimate purpose: to point forward to the coming day when, with the Word having become flesh, beauty itself would become incarnate to make all things new.

We cannot, then, get all the way by argument alone from the human perception and enjoyment of beauty to the existence or character of the Creator. But when, not least through the literary beauty of John's gospel, we are confronted with the beauty of redeeming love in the story of Jesus, we realize, looking back, that the signals we were receiving from all the beauty in the world were telling the truth.

John and the Jewish Festivals

One of the first things we realize, as we grasp the way John has laid out his book, is that he refers to the Jewish festivals more than all the other gospels put together. We'll look specifically at what John does with the Passover in the next chapter (on freedom), but here we shall examine two other major festivals that he highlights.

In chapter 7, it is time for the Festival of Tabernacles, and Jesus's family is going to Jerusalem. He gives them the impression that he won't be going, but after the others leave, he goes privately by himself. Tabernacles celebrates one particular aspect of the Exodus story, the time when the Israelites were living in the desert and God provided water for them out of the rock. Annual celebrations involved, among other things, the ceremonial pouring out of water in the Temple courtyard. It is in that context that Jesus gave his great invitation, echoing Isaiah 55:1: "If anybody's thirsty, they should come to me and have a drink!" (John 7:37). This, as we saw, was interpreted by John as referring to Jesus's promise of the Spirit.

Then, in chapter 10, it is winter in Jerusalem, and winter

means Hanukkah, the Festival of Lights. Part of the festivities at the time consisted of an eight-day celebration, giving rise to the eight candles that are lit to this day. This is the time when the Jewish people recall with thanksgiving the victory of Judas Maccabeus over the crazy Syrian emperor Antiochus Epiphanes. Antiochus swept through Judaea in 167 BC, took over the Temple, and desecrated it. This left the Judaeans with the choice of either compromise (abandoning their ancestral traditions) or rebellion.

Judas Maccabeus and his brothers, sons of a redoubtable old father, Mattathias, decided on rebellion. Three years later, in December 164, they won a famous victory, cleansed the Temple, and began to restore Israel in Judaea as once again the true people of the One God. Judas and his family, originally from the priestly line, became kings despite not being from the tribe of Judah or the family of David. They had other qualifications—they had cleansed the Temple and gotten rid of foreign oppressors, two rather obviously "messianic" tasks. Judas's descendants, called Hasmoneans, ruled Judaea for the next hundred years. When their line ran out and Herod the Great took over, he took care to marry a Hasmonean princess, Mariamne. He was claiming that he and his descendants would be the true "kings of the Jews."

This, then, sets the context for John 10, the Good Shepherd discourse. The use of the shepherd image for royalty is frequent in the ancient world. When Jesus talks of "all the people who came before me" as "thieves and brigands," this is pretty explicit language aimed at the Hasmoneans and Herodians and any other would-be messiah figures who showed up from time to time. They are all imposters, he says. They are like hired servants who won't actually face up to the real enemy. That is the context in which Jesus speaks of the "good shepherd"—the real, true, proper one—who lays down his life for the sheep. That, strangely but dramatically, is the one messianic qualification that will count.

Throughout this Johannine theme of the fulfillment of Israel's festivals it's clear what John is doing. He is telling the story of Jesus in such a way as to sum up the entire story of Israel: from Abraham through Moses through David and the prophets, up to and beyond the quite recent political turmoil that had shaped the Jewish world of his day. Jesus is where it was all going. It all came true in him—though in a way nobody had imagined in advance.

Chapter Five

Freedom

IN 2011 THERE WAS A SUDDEN MOVEMENT AMONG YOUNGER and better-educated people in north Africa and the Middle East. They wanted more freedom, more democracy, more women's rights, and so on. Western journalists labeled this the "Arab spring." Hillary Clinton, at that time the US Secretary of State, declared that the movement had to be supported, because it was "important to be on the right side of history." Somehow the Western powers had thought their way into a curious trap, a kind of low-grade version of Jean-Jacques Rousseau's diagnosis that "man is born free but is everywhere in chains" and Marx's prescription for breaking those chains. All you have to do is to topple a few dictators and then "freedom" will emerge as a raw, fresh product, creating a happier, more just, and equitable world. If only.

The Western powers, looking on, decided to intervene and

help the process, producing only more disasters. Now they have decided not to intervene elsewhere, and, at the time of this writing, we are still watching the consequences unfold. Freedom? Spring? Not much sign of either just now. Rather, there is confusion, helped on its way by shallow thinking from people who can then retreat to their Western security. *We all know freedom is important for human flourishing, but we all find it harder than we thought to see what it might mean or how to attain it.*

We see the same puzzles at the personal level. Old people like me smile when we see teenagers who, released from their childhood garb or their school uniforms, express their "freedom" by wearing identical jeans, T-shirts, and sneakers. Or, more darkly, by indulging in those well-known steps to "freedom"—tobacco, alcohol, harder drugs, and promiscuous sex. As we all know, the "freedom" to use drugs leads to slavery. And, as every counselor knows but many people prefer to forget, the freedom to engage in multiple romantic and/or sexual relationships works the same way. Once you are "hooked," you are quite seriously enslaved. Freedom in one direction is purchased at the specific cost of nonfreedom in another. Take your choice.

Our culture has thus been plagued with misunderstandings about freedom. Freedom *from* outer constraints isn't the same as freedom *for* some purpose or goal. The great philosophical debates about free will work the same way. Is everything we do, say, and think subtly "determined" by blind forces at work in our genes and our environment? Just because it *feels* as though I have the free choice to take this road to town or that road down to the sea, is that just an illusion?

Nobody actually lives as a strict determinist, of course; it would be difficult, especially once you realize that if everything you think is "conditioned" and "not free," then this thought too (the thought "I am not free, I am only thinking what I'm conditioned to think") is itself an unfree thought caused by, well, something else. Going down that road will make you crazy. But if, then, I am "free," does that mean I am like a random subatomic molecule, zipping around without apparent rhyme or reason? That is neither attractive nor really believable.

Widespread human experience suggests that freedom often emerges *through* a pathway that seems anything but "free." The freedom to improvise musically or to compose music of your own will only come when the disciplines of learning the scales and the technique for the instrument have been mastered. People sometimes imagine that when musicians improvise, as in jazz and other forms, they are just making up *anything*, playing the first thing that comes into their heads. They couldn't be more wrong. Jazz depends, just as much as classical music does, on the musicians knowing exactly what's going on, listening intently to one another, and making sure that even the most apparently daring riffs and outlandish extra passages come in to land at the right moment, in the right key. The music may sound strange to those unused to the idiom, but it has its own deep coherence. That is the difference between freedom and chaos.

So if we all know that freedom is important, socially and personally, but we all find it harder than we expected to figure out what it actually means, where do we go for help? The Bible shows us that our instinct for freedom has everything to do with the sense of the presence of God. Freedom, we find, is the central story God wants for his people—including both freedom *from* things like sin and idolatry and freedom *for* being loved. The story John tells in his gospel, like the story we find woven deep in the texture of Paul's thought, is the story of how the creator God has provided not only a new freedom, but a new *kind* of freedom. The Exodus, it turns out, is not only an event in Israel's past history, but a promise for the whole creation, a promise that Jesus makes real for all his followers.

The Passover Story of Freedom

It is a fact insufficiently acknowledged that the great overarching story of the Hebrew scriptures is the story of Israel's quest for freedom. Abraham's family faces many problems in Genesis and Exodus, but the big one is being enslaved in Egypt. The answer is the Exodus, celebrated every year at Passover. Thereafter the Jewish people were constantly reminded of the faithfulness of YHWH, in the scriptures, the Prophets and the Psalms, and in the annual festivals. Their God had performed great acts of liberation in the past, and he would do so again.

When we tell the story of the Jewish people in the centuries before Jesus's day, we often highlight the great political and social upheavals, the rise and fall of empires (Persia, Greece, Egypt, Syria, Rome). But we must never forget that in most Jewish families in most towns and villages, in both Judaea and Galilee and in the increasingly wide dispersion of Jewish people around the known world, minds would be formed day by day, month by month, and year by year not so much by reflection on the great powers that history records, but by the Sabbaths, the annual Passovers, the other festivals, and—when they could manage it—pilgrimages to Jerusalem itself. There they would celebrate in the city of David and pray for another David to arise, one who might make Passover happen again, one who might bring about a real new Exodus, a release from the present slavery once and for all.

John explains in chapter 2 that it was Passover time when Jesus came to Jerusalem. Like everything else in chapter 2 (the wedding at Cana and the demonstration in the Temple), this statement carries weight for the whole gospel. Passover was, and is, the greatest of the Jewish celebrations. In its origins and development it continued to have ancient associations with agriculture; the second day after Passover is the "offering of the first fruits," the bringing before God of the initial signs and hopes of a harvest to come. That, no doubt, is part of the reason why in the earliest church the resurrection of Jesus was celebrated as the "first fruits" of the coming "harvest" of the general resurrection and the entire new creation (see, e.g., 1 Cor. 15:20–28).

But Passover itself, the sacrificing of the lambs and the Festival of Unleavened Bread, had always been more than an agricultural festival. From Exodus 12 onward, it was the celebration of God's rescue of his people from slavery in Egypt. The Passover liturgy to this day rehearses the great story, from Moses's confrontation with Pharaoh and the plagues on Egypt to the crossing of the Red Sea and the journey in the wilderness with the promised land always in view. As a liturgical festival involving the whole family where possible, it has always etched into the minds of worshippers the belief that, through the covenant faithfulness of the Creator, Israel is a free people. Any subsequent slavery of any sort therefore represents a kind of category mistake, something God must sort out and put right sooner or later.

Thus, when Jews of Jesus's day congregated in Jerusalem to celebrate Passover, they were doing more than hoping for a good harvest later in the year. They were saying, "God set us free from slavery all those years ago, *and we are looking to him to do it again!*" That, no doubt, is the reason for the strange custom, which we meet in all four gospels, of the Roman governor releasing a prisoner at the people's request. It was a small sign, grudging perhaps on the part of the Romans—but they were pragmatic rulers—of the meaning of the festival. They let the Jews have a bit of "freedom" if it kept them quiet. One released prisoner wouldn't worry Caesar.

John mentions two more Passovers and exploits the significance of both. The first is the time in chapter 6 when Jesus feeds the large crowd in the desert (6:4). Throughout most of the long chapter, with its twists and turns of discussion about "bread from heaven," we are clearly meant to have the Exodus story in our heads. Jesus walks on the water, reminding the disciples of YHWH's conquest of the Red Sea (6:16–21). The people mention that Moses gave their ancestors bread from heaven in the desert; Jesus appears to do likewise (6:31–35). But Jesus is more than simply a prophet like Moses. He doesn't just *give* them bread. He *is* the bread. They don't understand. Nor will they, until the third and final Passover in the sequence.

It is of enormous importance for understanding Jesus and the whole early Christian movement that *Jesus chose Passover* to go to Jerusalem and do what had to be done. He did not choose any of the other festivals (nor indeed the great and solemn Day of Atonement) for this purpose.

The final Passover is introduced at 13:1, when John makes that the opening phrase of the second half of his gospel. There is a long-standing question as to whether John sees the Last Supper (with the foot washing) as a kind of Passover meal (which it clearly is in Mark, Matthew, and Luke) or whether—since the chronology is laid out quite carefully, with the Passover lambs being sacrificed as Jesus goes to his crucifixion—he sees the meal as simply preparatory. Perhaps he is suggesting that Jesus was deliberately celebrating the festival early. But that really isn't the point.

For John, as for all the early Christians, what Jesus did in going to the cross, and what the Father was declaring when he raised him from the dead, was a *Passover-shaped message*, the news that true freedom was being won at last, that the great Pharaoh had been overthrown, and that now it was time for the true Tabernacle to be built, for the true Torah to be kept, and for the ultimate inheritance to be claimed. All of that is going on underneath John's sequence of Passovers in his gospel, and the third one in particular.

Freedom from Sin and Idols

John's emphasis on the Passover repeatedly demonstrates God's commitment to freeing his people from outwardly oppressive rulers and systems, but God is concerned with the individual heart as well. We should not be surprised to find that internal freedom is a major theme in John—and a controversial one at that:

> Jesus spoke to the Judaeans who had believed in him.
> "If you remain in my word," he said, "you will truly be my disciples, and you will know the truth, and the truth will make you free."

"We are Abraham's descendants!" they replied. "We've never been anyone's slaves! How can you say, 'You'll become free'?"

"I'm telling you the solemn truth," Jesus replied. "Everyone who commits sin is a slave of sin. The slave doesn't live in the house forever; the son lives there forever. So, you see, if the son makes you free, you will be truly free." (8:31–36)

The whole second half of chapter 8, in fact, is about the question of the true children of Abraham (a question that continued to bother many in the early church, as Paul's letters to Galatia and Rome bear witness). But here it suddenly comes into focus in relation to the Exodus agenda, the freedom agenda. Jesus, faced with people who have "believed in him" up to this point, is explaining—or trying to explain—that he is indeed bringing about the long-awaited freedom, but that it won't look like what they expected.

Their initial reaction is astonishing: "We've never been anyone's slaves!" That is, of course, ridiculous. They are blustering. The whole point of Israel's central narrative, the Exodus story, is precisely that Israel *was* enslaved in Egypt. And the long, sorry story of Babylon and exile was another form of slavery, which was seen by many of Jesus's contemporaries as continuing in various forms up to and including his own day.

Jesus ignores these strange inconsistencies. He is making straight for a very different sort of "slavery." "Everyone who commits sin is a slave of sin," he says. At a stroke, he is translating the notion of slavery, so well known in the Jewish tradition (though apparently screened out by his present interlocutors), into a disease of the heart. He is not saying that "outward" slavery doesn't matter. Rather, exactly cognate with what he had said to Nicodemus, he is challenging his hearers to realize that there is a kind of slavery deep within the person, and that this form of slavery actually disqualifies one from being part of Abraham's true family. (That, I take it, is the point of saying that the slave does not ultimately belong in "the house.") So where has this idea of a new kind of slavery come from?

Like most of Jesus's other innovations, it emerges from many hints in Israel's scriptures themselves. The heart, said Jeremiah, is deceitful and desperately wicked (17:9). Jeremiah had seen that the real problem with the Israel of his day was not simply political weakness or bad leadership. It went much, much deeper. Jesus picks up on that elsewhere, warning about sicknesses of the heart, which produce things that make someone "unclean" (Mark 7:20–23).

Ezekiel too probes behind the outward problems that had led up to Israel's exile and defines the real need as a different *kind* of heart (Ezek. 36). Behind Jeremiah and Ezekiel stands Deuteronomy 30, which promises that when the Israelites turn back to God with their entire heart and soul, then God will "circumcise" their hearts so that they will love him and serve him truly. And that, granted the story in Deuteronomy 27–29, means that the slavery and exile that will come upon the people will be overcome at last. This, in other words, is the promise of the "new covenant," as in Jeremiah 31.

Jesus, here and elsewhere in John, clearly sees sin as something larger than simply individual wrong actions. Like Paul, he appears to understand sin as a *power*. We shall be looking at power more fully in the last chapter, but for the moment, to understand what is meant in this strange but important passage, we must say this. When someone sins, Jesus is saying, this isn't just a moral glitch. It is not simply about an occasional lapse or mistake. It is a sign that someone or something else is calling the shots. You may still have to agree to the impulses, but your resistance has been weakened. Your slave master has given the orders, and you find yourself driven helplessly down the wrong path. At a certain point you may even have convinced yourself that it is the right path, just as George Orwell's hero in *Nineteen Eighty-Four*, Winston Smith, eventually gave up the unequal struggle and simply loved Big Brother. That is what Jesus is talking about.

So what is this dark power that takes over people, that Jesus could see had taken over his own people, the people who prided themselves on being "children of Abraham"? The larger category in the scriptures that explains what is going on here is idolatry. Idols, all the more powerful when not recognized as such, are anything at all that humans place above and give their ultimate allegiance to other than the One God himself.

Why do we do this? Because idols always promise a bit extra— or perhaps a lot extra. An idol starts off as something good, a good part of God's good creation. But when it attracts attention and begins to offer more than it can appropriately deliver, it starts to demand sacrifices. You have to abandon part of your proper allegiance to God—and often to your neighbors, your family, your other duties—in order to give fresh and inappropriate attention to the new idol, whatever it is.

Idols are addictive. We know a good deal in our generation about the forms of addiction that are rife in our society. Far fewer people are addicted to cigarettes than was the case fifty years ago, but the same kind of compulsive behavior, and often the same kind of *destructive* behavior, is now associated not only with alcohol, cannabis, and other drugs, but with our electronic systems: smartphones, social media, Facebook, and so on. These, as is well known, can become *self*-destructive when people portray themselves in a particular light and then struggle to live up to the image they have created. These forms of addiction can become a classic example of Luther's definition of sin: "Humans turned in upon themselves." Technology can of course be a blessing, bringing people together in all sorts of ways, but in the last analysis real relationships with real people are a form of freedom. Half-relationships with a screen personality can be a step toward slavery.

These are our modern addictions, but there were ancient equivalents. As we look at Jesus's public career and see the challenge he issued, explicitly and implicitly, to his contemporaries, we can see what he might have been thinking of. At the heart of the cry for freedom among the Jews of Jesus's day was the longing to be politically independent, from Rome and everybody else. The best of Jesus's contemporaries would no doubt speak of cleansing the land, the city of Jerusalem, and above all the Temple from all foreign pollution, so that the Jews could be the holy people of God, which, at their best, they knew themselves called to be.

But that could easily slide, and no doubt frequently did, into the desire simply to be rid of foreigners, to be free from paying taxes, to live as proud, independent people—and to forget the vocation of Israel to be the light of the world, the "royal priesthood" chosen for the sake of the world, to bear witness to the God whom the prophets had promised would see his name reverenced beyond the borders of Israel (Mal. 1:5, 11, 14). There is such

Broken Signposts

a thing as idolatry of nationhood, and John describes the chief priests and the Pharisees expressing exactly that in chapter 11:

> "What are we going to do?" they asked. "This man is performing lots of signs. If we let him go on like this, everyone is going to believe in him! Then the Romans will come and take away our holy place, and our nation!"
>
> But one of them, Caiaphas, the high priest that year, addressed them.
>
> "You know nothing at all!" he said. "You haven't worked it out! This is what's best for you: let one man die for the people, rather than the whole nation being wiped out." (11:47–50)

One could suggest that the "holy place" was the real point of concern. But from what we know of the Jerusalem Temple in Jesus's day and what many other Jews thought of it, for the people in this scene it was very much the center of personal power rather than the place they went to meet with their holy and loving God, the Creator of all. It had become a symbol of national pride, status, and security. We know about that in our world, of course. It is a more or less universal human temptation. But we can see only too well in this story what it means to worship idols. It means being prepared to sacrifice humans if necessary. And those of us who have spent much of our lives working in church circles know that the same kind of temptation is always present to pastors, teachers, theologians, and other church leaders just as it is in other professions, only perhaps in church settings it takes an even uglier form because of what church leadership *ought* to be like if it was true to its calling.

128

Of course, as John goes on to point out, even the dark plotting of a cynic like Caiaphas was held within the larger saving purpose of God. The death that the chief priest was plotting for Jesus—getting rid of him, so that the nation as a whole would be saved—was a parody of the death to which Jesus himself believed himself called, called as the climax of his own scripture-fulfilling vocation: the death that would not only rescue the nation, but also "gather into one the scattered children of God" (11:52). There is the difference in a nutshell. Jesus's death was the ultimate in the self-giving love to which Israel's God was calling his true Son. Caiaphas meant it as the expression of his self-protective cynicism. The former led to freedom. The latter merely intensified the deepest form of slavery.

Our Free Identity in Christ

So what does Jesus mean by speaking of a "true" freedom? What does "knowing the truth" mean here, and how does that generate or sustain this different kind of freedom?

We shall be looking at truth in the next chapter, but for the moment we can say this. In John's gospel the truth, or knowing something "truly," regularly means probing down below the surface to see things the way God sees them. Mostly, this remains hidden; but Jesus is bringing it to light. And what comes to light is not just the diagnosis of the problem—the analysis of sin as a form of slavery, the sign that idols are being worshipped and that people are in their grip. There is also the remedy. The powers are to be defeated. And when that is done, through Jesus's death, those who have been held captive by them can be released at last.

What will that look like? Returning to Nicodemus, it will mean a new kind of birth, a new, true way to be human. John's gospel is all about Genesis and new Genesis: Genesis 1 focuses on the human beings who are to bear the divine image, and John's gospel explains how it is that the True Image-Bearer, Jesus himself, enables others to become genuine humans at last. This is the answer to the desperate and often tortured longings of so many today, in the parts of the world that are hurting badly from poverty, disease, and war, but also in the parts of the world that live in an empty luxury that has forgotten the point of life. The true human identity comes from the True Human himself: if the Son makes you free, you will be truly free.

Back too to the woman of Samaria. She was enslaved by her past, by her own sin and that of many others—so many layers of bad memories, of bad mental and physical habits. Every time she managed to break out of one destructive situation, she was instantly lured to find another one to get stuck in. That is a syndrome as well known as the weather and as wide as the world. And Jesus is offering a way out, a true freedom, a genuinely fresh start.

To understand why that might be available and how it is put into operation, you need to read the story through to the end. Then, like Mary, Thomas, and Peter in John 20–21, you need to respond appropriately to the Jesus who has dealt with the sorrow, doubt, and denial of the past and now welcomes you into a new world. And as we respond we discover, as one old song put it, that "freedom" means "the time I've been loved." Something about love—anyone's love—creates a kind of freedom, a new space, a larger world. Something about God's love becoming human in Jesus and dying on the cross brings about a new creation, and invites each of us to inhabit it. A new world. A free world. Free people within a free world.

Free people, then, become agents of freedom in the world, at every level: counselors who help others to shake off the shackles of the past and live in genuine freedom, diplomats who confront bullying and tyrannical rulers with the news that there is a better way to run countries or systems, politicians who craft legislation that sets ordinary people free from clever bullies, and so on. In all this we are once again coming around the corner to the theological point. The desire for freedom is a God-given instinct implanted in all image-bearers. The God who made us *wants us to be free.*

Of course in many systems—tragically, in many would-be Christian systems and churches—that message has been totally squelched under a large, heavy pile of regulations and expectations. Many people will find any association of "freedom" with "church" like yet another of Sartre's sick jokes. But it isn't. The church at its best—and I have been privileged to glimpse some of that "best"—is in the freedom business, at every level.

This shows, yet again, that the call of freedom, though it appears to run into the sand in so many contexts, was always a genuine call from the creator God. The instinct that causes even tyrants to claim that they are offering people "freedom," the instinct that tells people to break out of their straitjackets and find a new liberty—this instinct is part of the genuine, God-given kit for human life. That remains true however much we abuse it, however much we take the promise of freedom and twist it into new forms of slavery. The broken signpost is still a signpost.

Look at it like this, anticipating some of what we will be

looking at in the last two chapters. On the night Jesus was betrayed, Peter followed him all the way to the high priest's hall. He was free not to go, but he went out of loyalty. Once there, he was free to agree with the bystanders that he was one of Jesus's followers, and he was also free to deny it. He denied it. And once he had used his "freedom" that way, *he was no longer free*. He was crushed by his mistake, by the way his proud boasting of a few hours earlier had been shown up—as Jesus warned him would happen—as hollow. So after his resurrection Jesus gave Peter back his freedom—by forgiving him, by inviting his love, and by commissioning him to take over the role of shepherd.

Oh, and one other thing. Peter's new freedom would lead him to a place that would look like the very opposite of freedom: to suffering and death. The paradox of freedom, it seems, continues in a new mode. But the conversation ends with Jesus saying, "Follow me." Jesus himself was the most free person who has ever walked the earth, and his freedom led him to crucifixion. That is because, once more, freedom grows out of love. If you want to know what freedom really means, think of the time you've been loved. Of the time when the Son of God loved you and gave himself for you. Of the time when God so loved the world that he gave his only Son.

On Reading John and Listening for Jesus

By now some readers may feel overwhelmed with all the different themes and ideas that are packed so tightly together in John's gospel. I have taken particular ideas as starting points, but these awaken all sorts of echoes, and they bring other themes with them as well. There is always the danger that this kind of intense reading all becomes a blur, and particularly that the central character, Jesus himself, seems to get lost behind a flurry of words. But there are ways of making sure that doesn't happen. In this moment, in between freedom and truth, I want to explore one of them.

I said before that the conversations between Jesus and various people in John's gospel—much fuller and more wide-ranging than any conversations in the other three gospels—give us a strong sense of what Jesus was like as a person, as a friend, as someone you could talk to, even though he might frequently switch tracks and answer the question you *should* have asked instead of the one you actually did. And I've said that reading these stories encourages us to treat him like that in real life too. Jesus is alive and real.

When he calls his followers "friends" in John 15 and elsewhere, he clearly intends that circle of friends to grow, to include us today.

But suggesting that we could have conversations with Jesus *rather like* those conversations in the gospel only goes so far. What if we could actually become part of those conversations? Supposing we could join in?

Many readers will be familiar with this idea. Some, in fact, may have learned it as a way of reading the gospels before they began to read them any other way. But it bears repeating, because others may not have heard of it, and even those who have may value a reminder.

It's all about bringing prayer and scripture reading together in a fresh way. When you read the Bible you ought, in any case, to be laying yourself open to whatever God wants to say to you. But this requires that you go on the initiative. You pray for God's Spirit to guide you. You take, shall we say, that remarkable story of Jesus and Nicodemus and, in prayer, you say to Jesus, "D'you mind if I come in on this?" Nicodemus may be surprised; but if Jesus is happy (which he will be), Nicodemus has no cause for complaint.

So you join the conversation. This is the point where the line between prayer and imagination becomes thin to a vanishing point. (And yes, I know that imagination can then take over and lead you into mere fantasy. That's always a danger. But the imagination too is a gift from God to be used prayerfully.) So you listen, respectfully, as Nicodemus asks Jesus his opening question and Jesus replies to a different one. This happens a lot with Jesus, but you learn to go with it. He cuts to the heart of it: being born from above is what counts in God's kingdom. Nicodemus has obvious questions: How can an old person be born again? Jesus responds, talking about water and Spirit. More questions, more answers. Then, before it gets any more complicated, they both pause for breath. Now it's your turn. What did *you* have on your heart and mind as you listened to what's been said so far?

You might want to say, "Hold on a moment! Just explain that water-and-Spirit stuff again." Or you might want to say, "I thought I'd been 'born again' when I said a special prayer many years ago, but now I don't know where I'm at." Or perhaps you would want to ask, "What exactly did you mean, Jesus, when you spoke about the 'son of man' who had come down from heaven?" And if you ask those questions seriously and prayerfully, there is no knowing what answers you may receive.

But there's no reason to confine yourself to things Nicodemus and Jesus were talking about. Nicodemus came to Jesus by night, presumably because he didn't want to be seen. What is there about your life—and what is there about Jesus!—that might make *you* want to come to him secretly, without anybody knowing? What would you really want to ask him about? Jesus isn't fussy about the time of day. Come in the dark if that's what you need to do.

Or take two other scenes. In John 2 Jesus, his mother, and his friends go to a wedding where the wine runs out. Mary tells Jesus, and Jesus knows at once that she is suggesting he do something about it. So allocate yourself a walk-on part in that scene—only, instead of the wine running out at that wedding, think of the difficulties a couple you know are having in their marriage, perhaps, even, the difficulties you are having in *yours*. If there's a disaster looming, for whatever reason, tell Jesus about it. Bring it explicitly to his attention. Be a bit forward, as Mary obviously was. Confront him with what's going on.

Stay in the scene and watch what he does. It may be something quite unexpected, like when he told the servants to fill the large pots with water and bring them into the feast. Jesus has his own ways of addressing practical questions as well as theological ones. The important thing is that someone—in this case, you—is telling him what's happened, what the problem is, and that that "someone" needs to remember to respond to Mary's order, "Do whatever he tells you" (2:5).

Another intimate and moving story is the foot-washing scene in John 13. Read the story through till you know it well. Sense the puzzlement in the room as Jesus gets up from the table and begins to do what a servant would normally do. Listen to Peter, protesting that Jesus shouldn't be doing such a thing and then changing his tone when Jesus tells him it's essential (Peter replies, "Not only my feet—wash my hands and my head as well!").

What are *you* going to say when he comes around to you, gently removes your sandals, and begins to wash your feet? Which other bits of you need to be washed? Tell him about them and wait for his reply. Which deep griefs, fears, old sins, and failed hopes will his simple action bring to light? Explain it all to him as he wipes your feet with the towel. Wait while he dries your tears as well.

Chapter Six

Truth

T WO FRIENDS OF MINE WROTE A BOOK SOME YEARS AGO
with a challenging title: *Truth Is Stranger Than It Used to
Be.* Brian Walsh and Richard Middleton had wrestled for years
with the challenge of postmodernity. They had seen how the
students with whom they worked had come up against what
my friends described as the "socially constructed character of
reality." What they meant is that the big stories we were all told
now seemed to be a bunch of self-serving lies—including the
big story about how the scientific advances of the eighteenth
and nineteenth century meant that the Western world was now
leading human civilization and all the rest had to do was to
catch up. We—the West—had flattered ourselves that we were
the "good guys." But as we looked around the world, we saw
the devastating results of our efforts to "help" the rest of the
world get the point.

So is the big story a lie? Is there any such thing as truth anymore? Has it come to this—that powerful people "make their own truth," and everyone else has to put up with it?

Consider the case of a witness in court. In Britain to this day, witnesses have to swear a solemn oath that they will tell "the truth, the whole truth, and nothing but the truth." But every judge and every wise jury member will realize that this is an unattainable ideal. We know what is meant: the witness must not try to deceive either by adding extra bits, omitting key facts, or distorting what is described.

But it is obviously impossible to tell "the whole truth" in the sense of *everything that happened that day.* You'd be there for weeks, describing every breath you took, every passing car, every fly that buzzed past your nose. And if you tried to do that, the things that really mattered would get lost in a vast blur of irrelevant details. "The whole truth" can only really mean "the whole *relevant* truth."

But once we say that, we face the question: Who says what's relevant? Often the key events only come out through long cross-examination, as the trial lawyer probes into the memory and the witness finally mentions something that hadn't seemed important but now turns out to be crucial.

So here is the problem. All truth is "somebody's truth." Everything depends on who's telling the story and from what angle. But does that mean there's no such thing as truth after all? No, of course not. *That* man really was driving *that* car when it swerved and hit the pedestrian. The fact that one of the witnesses, his memory shaken and scarred by the horror of it all, misremembered the color of the car doesn't mean that nothing happened. It doesn't mean that we will never discover who was driving the car. It just means that human perception and memory are more complicated than we might have imagined.

And this is the way in which truth joins our other themes— justice, love, spirituality, beauty, and freedom. *We all know truth matters, but we've discovered it's not as easy to find or know as we thought.* It is a broken signpost. We yearn for truth—we need it—yet its perfection is always beyond our reach.

Ironically, the last few decades have seen a massive rise in the demand for "truth" in the form of official paperwork to be filled out (or "filled in," as we say in Britain). I travel a certain amount for work, and I've noticed how over recent decades I have had to fill out more and more official forms, send photographs of myself here and there, and now—in a recent and time-consuming procedure—have my fingerprints taken at certain border crossings. This, you could say, is a *modernist* reaction to a *postmodern* problem: postmodernity throws a choking blanket of suspicion over everybody and everything, so we respond with heavy-handed and cumbersome bureaucracy. After all, who knows, you might be a terrorist—so we'd better take your fingerprints!

You could sketch an entire theory about the problems of being human based on our desire for truth and our inability to get it. We demand more and more truth in the form of "facts," of completed official forms in the filing cabinet, but truth itself then becomes more and more demanding as people select and arrange the "facts" to fit the profile they want to create—the profile of events, the profile of the world, and particularly the profile of themselves. I once talked with a man who had applied for a particular job. He told me, in some detail, that he'd been offered the position, but that he had turned it down because he didn't much like the new colleagues he would have. What he didn't know—and I didn't tell him—was that I knew some of the colleagues in question, and I had heard, let us say, another side to the story.

And that's the trouble: so many stories have more than one side, more than two sides in fact. They have as many "sides" as there are pairs of eyes watching, minds ticking, and tongues talking. When I lived for a few months in the Middle East in 1989, I kept my eyes and ears open and did my best to understand the complexities of the political situation. I found everyone more or less convincing—but every account I heard was more or less incompatible with every other one. How does this happen? What should we do about it?

"We deceive ourselves," says John in his first letter, "and the truth is not in us" (1 John 1:8). And yet we know that we are called to be truth-telling creatures. We certainly want everyone else to tell the truth, and we are cross when they don't—especially the politicians and businesspeople who cook the books for profit while the people they are supposed to be serving pick up the tab.

And yet we deceive ourselves very easily, including telling lies about telling lies ("It wasn't really a lie"). Our highly selective memories pick out and highlight the tiny number of facts from the millions available to back up the picture we have of ourselves, our lives, and our behavior. This can of course itself go a different route. People who are inclined to depression or feelings of guilt may only remember the "facts" that fuel their sense of despair and shame. Truth itself seems as far away as the farthest star. But we still gaze at it in wonder. It is a thing of beauty—or so it seems.

The Christian gospel, however, offers a deeper approach to

truth than the world is able to provide. In a world where it is suggested that truth itself is an illusion—where truth itself seems like a broken signpost, leading us around in self-defeating circles—the followers of Jesus ought to respond that to proclaim the absence of truth is itself a lie. There is such a thing as truth, even if it's more elusive and strange than we sometimes imagine. What's more, it is the truth that will set us free—free to live as new creations and free to become truth tellers in our own right.

"Truth!" said Pilate. "What's That?"

John's gospel focuses at key points on the question of truth. "The law, you see, was given through Moses," says John cryptically near the end of the prologue (1:17); "grace and truth came through Jesus the Messiah." That's an interesting combination, "grace and truth." Perhaps John is hinting that there is indeed such a thing as truth, but that it takes grace not only to reveal it, but to *make it happen in the first place.* There is a reality toward which the whole created order is tending, but until the coming of Messiah Jesus it remains just out of reach, though Moses and the others are pointing to it.

This is a radical point, because throughout the Gospel of John we see Jesus interacting with various individuals whose words or actions challenge the idea that real truth exists. This reaches its notorious climax when Jesus is brought before the Roman governor on a charge of sedition. In a sense, the charge is true: if the present world is all that there is, then anyone who says there is a new world and that it's breaking into the present world, bringing life and hope instead of death and despair, is a dangerous fool leading the people astray. Much better to stick with the power structure you know: "We have no king except Caesar" (19:15). Caesar may kill you but, hey, you know where you are. (And the chief priests, who made that extraordinary claim, knew that Caesar was keeping them in power.)

But Jesus, at the climax of the gospel, speaks of creation and new creation:

> "So!" said Pilate. "You *are* a king, are you?"
>
> "You're the one who's calling me a king," replied Jesus. "I was born for this; I've come into the world for this: to give evidence about the truth. Everyone who belongs to the truth listens to my voice."
>
> "Truth!" said Pilate. "What's that?" (19:37–38)

This exchange is prompted by Jesus's saying that his kingdom is "not the sort that comes from here"; it is a different kind of kingdom. But it's a kingdom nonetheless, a kingdom that challenges the kingdom of Caesar, which Pilate of course represents, at a far more fundamental level than any armed rebellion ever could. Caesar's kingdom is held in place precisely by death, whether threatened or actual, in other words by the denial of the goodness of the creation.

This situation is what people mean when they say that empires "make their own truth." It's what Pilate meant when, with his cynical question, he anticipated today's postmodern protest ("There's no such thing as absolute truth") or the equivalent response made by those in power ("Truth? That's just fake news!"). Whatever doesn't fit the agenda can be waved away. I am reminded of how, when Russian troops took over the Crimea and the Ukraine was powerless to resist, Vladimir Putin went on television to say that the soldiers in question were local militias who had bought Russian military uniforms from secondhand shops.

Another famous conversation that helps us to pinpoint what Christianity says about truth has made many in our world shake their heads at its apparent arrogance. Thomas, puzzled as usual by Jesus's words, asks Jesus where he is going and how they can know the way. "I am the way," replies Jesus, "and the truth and the life!" (14:6). Some have read this as a Jewish way of saying "I am the true and living way," and that may be right as well. But the emphasis seems to me to fall equally on all three nouns, "way," "truth," and "life."

This extraordinary claim should not be heard so much within the sounding chamber of our modern world, where "truth" is the arrogant claim of the powerful. Truth here is the strange, gentle yet also powerful truth of new creation, the new creation that fulfills the old by taking the shame and death of the old into itself and overcoming it. Truth is the reality of love, divine love, Jesus's love, the Love made flesh.

This is not a claim to be measured alongside others, as though Jesus and half a dozen other teachers or leaders were being weighed against some arbitrary modern standard of "religion." Either Israel is the people of the creator God, or Israel is not; either Jesus is Israel's Messiah, or he is not. Either the creator God launched his new creation in and through Jesus as Israel's Messiah, or he did not. John's gospel is written to affirm all three propositions: Israel is God's people, Jesus is Israel's Messiah, and through him God has set in motion his new creation. And, not surprisingly, John's gospel is where Jesus constantly repeats the word "truly." In older translations it appears as "Truly, truly I say to you," and though I have translated it as "I'm telling you the solemn truth" (e.g., 14:12), the emphasis is the same.

What we've seen in Jesus's conversations with Pilate and Thomas is that truth, as the gospel defines it, is a reality, a unique reality, a reality somehow wrapped up in the person of Jesus. It is the truth of a different sort of kingdom altogether. One final piece of the puzzle becomes clearer in Jesus's conversation with the Samaritan woman. She asks Jesus for the "living water" he's talking about (4:15), and he responds by telling her to call her husband and come back. Quickly she replies (What is she thinking? What is John wanting us to think she's thinking?), "I haven't got a husband." (Perhaps this intriguing stranger might be interested?) Jesus slices through the half-truth, or half-lie:

> You're telling me you haven't got a husband! The fact is, you've had five husbands, and the one you've got now isn't your husband. You were speaking the truth! (4:17–18)

The irony is obvious: she was telling a half-truth with the intent to deceive, but inside that there really was a truth, even though it was the truth she didn't want Jesus to know. Instead, he challenges her to a different kind of truth, the truth that comes through worshipping the true God:

> The time is coming—indeed, it's here already!—when true worshippers will worship the father in spirit and in truth. Yes: that's the kind of worshippers the father is

looking for. God is spirit, and those who worship him must worship in spirit and in truth. (4:23–24)

So how does truth relate to worship? What is going on? How does *this* new kind of truth—the truth of God, the truth of genuine worship—reset the dial for all the truth we find so puzzling? We saw when discussing spirituality that, for this Samaritan woman, worship had been tied for generations to a particular place, while Jesus was instead calling her to embrace something new: to receive the living water that only he could offer, but that was not tied to particular sacred geography. A new sort of truth is being born into the world, but it will take a new sort of wisdom to discern and follow it. And this in turn will lead to confrontation.

Confronting the Father of Lies

Jesus's promise of truth takes us out of the purely private sphere and into the dangerous world of public truth, public truth claims, and the violence that lies ready to hand when those truth claims collide. This takes us back to John 8, the passage we looked at before in connection with freedom. Freedom and truth, it seems, go together:

"If you remain in my word," said Jesus, "you will truly be my disciples, and you will know the truth, and the truth will make you free." (8:31–32)

This produces an angry reaction, as we saw. But Jesus sticks to his point. He has told the truth, and they are telling lies. This can only mean one thing—that their refusal to believe him must come from a dark source, the source of all lies. Our ingrained mental habits will lead us to be suspicious of such suggestions. They appear self-serving. We shudder at the thought of "demonizing" our opponents. But suppose what Jesus says about truth and lies is really the truth?

> Why don't you understand what I'm saying? It can only be because you can't hear my word. You are from your father—the devil! And you're eager to get on with what he wants. He was a murderer from the beginning, and he's never remained in the truth, because there is no truth in him. When he tells lies, he speaks what comes naturally to him, because he is a liar—in fact, he's the father of lies! But because I speak the truth, you don't believe me. Which of you can bring a charge of sin against me? If I speak the truth, why don't you believe me? The one who is from God speaks God's words. That's why you don't listen, because you're not from God. (8:43–47)

This is perhaps the darkest point in John's gospel. Those of us who would never dream of saying anything like this to anyone, who like to "think the best of people," and who are aware of the deep ambiguity of all human life, including our own, may well find ourselves thinking that this is totally over the top. At first hearing, it sounds like a fundamentalist rant. In our eyes, it doesn't sit well between "God so loved the world" in chapter 3 and "I am the good shepherd" in chapter 10. (And if someone said that John 8 was their favorite part of the Bible, I think we would start to worry about their state of mind and heart.) But part of Christian humility is to put aside instant reactions to the parts of scripture that seem alien, and even alienating, and to pay attention to what is actually going on.

The drama of John's gospel, as we have seen, brings the huge story of God and the world into the sharp focus of the story of Jesus and Israel. It's there in the prologue. First, "He was in the world, and the world was made through him, and the world did not know him"; and then, bringing that down to the specific drama of this book, "He came to what was his own, and his own people did not accept him" (1:10–11). This is framed, silhouetted we might say, by the bright light from behind: "The light shines in the darkness, and the darkness did not overcome it" (1:5). There is, after all, such a thing as evil. The instinct not to give it its proper name is one of the tactics that evil itself employs in order to smuggle in its deadly purposes under the noses of those who, not themselves in the grip of evil, are nevertheless unwilling to confront it for fear of looking arrogant, of causing too much of a fuss.

But the world of lies is the world of death, and sooner or later we have to face up to that. *Death itself tells lies about God and about Jesus.* The good world, which the Father made through the agency of the Word, is indeed good, and the corruption, decay, and death that infect it and declare that it's all deceitful trash are themselves deceitful trash. *No,* God replies, *this is my world; I love it and I am rescuing it.* Death sneers in the face of God. Jesus weeps in the face of death. And on Easter Day Mary's tears are turned to joy because truth itself is reborn, the truth that this *is* after all the Creator's world and that he *has* rescued it and *is* renewing it.

In the light of that larger story, truth must be told that will confront lies and hold them up to shame. Only so will people be set free from the grip of the lie. But how? The greatest crimes of the twentieth century—the Turkish massacre of Armenians, the Nazi massacre of Jews, and Pol Pot's massacre of his political opponents and anyone else in the way—were able to happen because people who knew about them didn't speak up. Many politicians have discovered that people will detect and confront a small lie, but if you tell a really big lie (think of Hitler telling the German people that Winston Churchill was aiming at world domination), people will either not notice or assume it must somehow be true, despite appearances.

So Jesus confronts his opponents as they are confronting him. (Their response, not for the first time, is to accuse him of being demon-possessed.) The truth he is telling simply won't fit into their models of how the world works. They are frantically shoring up the world the way they see it.

The sign that their agenda is driven by the dark anticreation power is that they too want to use violence. The chapter begins with the threat to stone the adulterous woman, and it ends with the attempt to stone Jesus (8:59). This is all part of the buildup to the climax of the gospel, when again the question of truth and falsehood stands right beside the question of life and death. Gradually the point emerges. *The reason truth is such a paradox in the present time is that the ultimate truth is the new creation, which fulfills the present creation by abolishing death, which has corrupted it.* No wonder the forces of darkness, of anticreation, the diabolical, accusing forces, shriek and snarl and throw stones.

The New Truth of Love

So what might it mean that Jesus's kingdom both comes from somewhere else and is characterized by a level of truth telling that goes far deeper than the lies and sneers of the world?

The new world that comes into being with Jesus's work and will arrive in a whole new way through his death and resurrection is the real new creation for which the first creation had been longing all the time. Jesus's proposals for God's kingdom coming "on earth as in heaven" were not about a quirky, bizarre counterculture that might attract by its novelty but wouldn't actually mesh with the long hopes and aspirations—the desire for justice, love, spirituality, beauty, and freedom—of ordinary human hearts and minds. It was about the genuine creation, free at last from corruption, decay, and death itself, that would satisfy those longings. It was about the Creator's ultimate purposes being fulfilled. Truth as we find it in this world is only a broken signpost. The Pilates and chief priests of this world have knocked it out of line. We don't trust it anymore. But the longing for truth and our half-hearted attempts at it turn out in retrospect to be genuine signposts to ultimate reality.

But the fact that the kingdom comes from somewhere else— from God himself, obviously—rather than being created from within the present world, speaks powerfully of what this truth really is and how it comes into being. John has been telling us throughout his gospel that the Creator, the God of Abraham, to whom Jesus bears witness and whom he claims in some strange sense even to embody, is the God of *love*. Creation itself was made through love and will be remade through love. It is love that washes the disciples' feet. It is love that invites them to share the intimacy of relation that exists even between the Father and the Son. It is love that goes to the cross.

And that is why Pilate's "truth"—the truth of empire, the truth that comes out of the scabbard of a sword (or, as we would say, out of the barrel of a gun)—can only ever be the half-truth that, when made into a whole truth, becomes an untruth. Yes, that is the way the world is at present. *But it's not the way it was meant to be, and it's not the way it's going to be.*

If you collude with Pilate's truth, you are becoming part of the "people of the lie," the people who do deals with death itself, as Jesus charges in John 8:39–47. And this leads us to the deepest mystery of all, which is close to the heart of what later theologians loosely refer to as "atonement."

The long argument between Jesus and Pilate, after all, appears to end in Pilate's victory. He has the power to crucify Jesus, and Jesus acknowledges that he really does have that power (19:11). And he exercises that power. He tries to remove the signs of truth, as people of the lie always do, in this case the person who is telling the uncomfortable truth. But since the ultimate truth is the self-giving love that made the world and will remake the world, Pilate thereby undermines his own lie.

The darkness overreaches itself. The power of death is lured to the place where death itself will be defeated. As Paul puts it in 1 Corinthians 2:8, if the rulers of the world had realized what they were doing, they would never have crucified the Lord of Glory. They were signing their own death warrant. "Death shall be no more," declared the poet John Donne. "Death, thou shalt die."

That is the truth the Gospel of John is declaring in the confrontation between Caesar's spokesman and God's. For the new creation of truth and love to be born, the ultimate corruption that has infected the present creation must be allowed to do its worst and thereby exhaust itself. John's way of telling the whole story of Jesus indicates that this is how he is reading the great scriptural narrative of creation and Israel, of Israel and the coming Messiah. What the Messiah achieves is the true truth, the creational truth, the new-creational truth.

Truth-telling Jesus Followers

Jesus's followers will therefore be commissioned to be people of the truth. This will be immensely costly for them, as it was for him. But they will be directed into this vocation by the Spirit himself, now designated precisely as "the spirit of truth":

> "If you love me," Jesus went on, "you will keep my
> commands. And I will ask the father, and he will give you
> another helper, to be with you forever. This other helper
> is the spirit of truth. The world can't receive him, because
> it doesn't see him or know him. But you know him,
> because he lives with you, and will be in you." (14:15–17)

This new Spirit, Jesus's own Spirit, will come and enable them to tell the truth, particularly to tell the world the truth about Jesus himself, the truth that doesn't fit into the old world but that makes ultimate, radical, and renewing sense of that old world:

> When the helper comes—the one I shall send you
> from the father, the spirit of truth who comes from the

father—he will give evidence about me. And you will give evidence as well, because you have been with me from the start. (15:26–27)

In other words, *truth itself will come to birth as Jesus's followers speak the words that bring the new creation into existence.* This is the exciting new vocation that makes sense of our puzzles about truth in philosophy and culture. The truth of new creation, which flows outward from the truth of Jesus, his kingdom, his death, and his resurrection, makes its way not least through the truth telling of Jesus's followers. This cannot collapse back into the rationalism or modernism of some Christian expressions of "truth," the brittle attempts to "prove" the gospel through arguments that (apparently) only a fool would deny. What Jesus is talking about will include the telling of his own story, of course, but that storytelling, like Jesus's own storytelling, will be the inner explanation for the larger goal of truth *living*, bringing the healing and hope of new creation in all directions.

This means, as we would have guessed from the commissioning in 20:19–23, that the Spirit will enable Jesus's followers to be for the world what Jesus was for Israel. And this in turn will mean that, far from leaving behind the story of who precisely he was and what he did in his public career, that must remain central. At the heart of the church's truth telling will be its true telling of the story of Jesus himself. The Spirit will help the church to go on telling this story and telling it properly:

"There are many things I still have to say to you," Jesus continued, "but you're not yet strong enough to take them. When the spirit of truth comes, though, he will

guide you in all the truth. He won't speak on his own
account, you see, but he will speak whatever he hears.
He will announce to you what's to come. He will glorify
me, because he will take what belongs to me and will
announce it to you. Everything that the father has is mine.
That's why I said that he would take what is mine and
announce it to you." (16:12–15)

And this is in keeping with the prayer Jesus prays at the conclusion of the discourses:

I'm not asking that you should take them out of the world,
but that you should keep them from the evil one. They
didn't come from the world, just as I didn't come from the
world. Set them apart for yourself in the truth; your word
is truth. Just as you sent me into the world, so I sent them
into the world. And on their account I set myself apart
for you, so that they too many be set apart for you in the
truth. (17:15–19)

Set them apart for yourself in the truth; your word is truth. The word
for "set apart" is the same as the word for "sanctify"; here Jesus's
followers are being set apart for God's special use, like the ves-
sels in the Tabernacle. In the High-Priestly Prayer of John 17,
Jesus is there, in the Father's intimate presence, embodying the
truth of new creation, the truth toward which the Tabernacle
and Temple had always pointed, and praying that this truth, this
new reality, will clothe his followers, so that they will be bathed
in it, formed by it, and able to live it, breathe it, and speak it into
the world, the world into which they are sent.

Here we find a powerful resolution to the problem with which we began, the problem of the paradox of truth in today's world. The notion of truth itself, and the way in which it slips through our fingers precisely when we want it most, might lead us to despair; it certainly leads many today into forms of cynicism. By itself, in fact, the human quest for truth is a battered and broken signpost: one could be forgiven for supposing, with Pilate, that all it deserves is a cynical shrug of the shoulders.

But, though Pilate would never understand it, Truth was standing before him, the truth of creation rescued and renewed, truth turned into flesh, Truth loving his own who were in the world and now loving them to the uttermost, Truth leading the way through death and out the other side into God's new world, giving his followers the Spirit of truth, so that they could come after him and speak the creative truth that will bring that world into being. Part of the challenge of following Jesus is to learn the difficult, dangerous but beautiful art of speaking fresh, healing truth into the world that often still seems to be ruled by Caesar's agents.

Who, Then, Is Jesus?

John's gospel is famous for the "I am" sayings of Jesus. We just mentioned one: "I am the way and the truth and the life" (14:6). The others belong within various settings: "I am the bread of life" (6:35, 48); "I am the light of the world" (8:12; 9:5); "I am the good shepherd" (10:11, 14); "I am the resurrection and the life" (11:25); "I am the true vine" (15:1). Many have seen the "I am" in these sayings as a deliberate echo of the divine name, as in Exodus 3:14 ("I AM WHO I AM," then shortened simply to "I AM").

John appears to make this direct connection; in two different scenes Jesus refers to himself simply as "I am." It is always ambiguous in the Greek, since the Greek, *egō eimi*, is also a natural way of saying, "It's me" or "I'm the one." We find this ambiguity when Jesus is walking on the water and the disciples are terrified (6:19–20), and we rightly interpret what Jesus says as, "It's me!" But John, equally rightly, is hinting that this is Israel's God in person, striding over the stormy waves.

We find this again in the Garden of Gethsemane, when Jesus, utterly vulnerable before the approaching band of soldiers and police, asks them who they are looking for. When they say,

"Jesus of Nazareth," he simply replies, "I am" (18:5, 6, 8). The first time he says it, the soldiers step back and fall to the ground. John seems quite deliberate in implying that the presence of Jesus in the darkened garden is to be understood as the strange divine Presence envisaged in Israel's scriptures.

But what do we conclude from these two examples? For many years these texts have been interpreted to mean that Jesus was supposedly "claiming to be God." In the light of the famous opening of the gospel ("In the beginning was the Word . . . and the Word was God"), this naturally seems to make sense. But this idea of "claiming to be God" has too often been framed within the debates of modern Western thought in which "God" was increasingly a philosopher's god, a Deist god perhaps, a distant, aloof being. Many philosophers and theologians during the last few centuries have assumed that, in order to expound or commend the Christian faith, their task was to "prove" the existence of God—in some way or other—and then to fit Jesus into this picture. John's gospel appeared to give them the tools for the latter task, because here indeed was Jesus "claiming to be God."

But John himself indicates that this is the wrong way of going about things. Starting with God and hoping then to fit Jesus into the picture is putting the cart before the horse. "Nobody has ever seen God," he insists. "The only-begotten God, who is intimately close to the father—he has brought him to light" (1:18). This is an extraordinary claim. We do not, he insists, know ahead of time who the true God really is. We can't get a "fix" on God and then hope to slot Jesus into the model we have constructed. It will never work that way. We must always start with Jesus and allow him to do what he did with everything else he touched, and indeed what he did in every conversation he had—to reshape the discourse, to reorder the world, and in this case to remake the very notion of God around his own extraordinary sense of vocation.

There should be no question that John *does* want to say that in some sense Jesus is God; "The Word was God" in the first verse is quite explicit. Don't be fooled by those who claim that in the Greek it says, "The Word was *a* god." There is no *a* in the Greek, because that's not how Greek works. Greek regularly has the definite article (our "the") for the *subject* of a sentence that involves the verb "to be," and equally regularly it omits it for the *complement*, the thing that is being said about the subject. If we were to translate the sentence "Elizabeth is the queen" into Greek, the Greek equivalent of "the" would go with "Elizabeth" as the subject, not "queen." In Greek it would look like, "The Elizabeth is queen." This little grammatical footnote simply underlines the fact that John tells us up front that the "Word," who later at a point in time "became flesh," is God. In other words, without getting too technical, within the unity of the creator God there is (at least, and to put it nontechnically) something of a bipolarity.

This would not have been a shock to most Jewish monotheists of the time. The idea of monotheism was not, in Jesus's day, a philosophical analysis of the "inner being" of the One God. It was a strong affirmation of two things. First, the world was made by a single good and wise creator. This rules out any suggestion of a "dualism" in which the created order might be the lesser, or indeed evil, creation of a lesser, or indeed evil, divinity.

Second, this creator is the *only* God; in other words, the many so-called gods and lords of the pagan pantheon are just a sham.

Any power they appear to have is due to irritating but ultimately trivial "demons" who exploit humans by luring them into worshipping the nongods like Zeus, Athena, and the rest.

So it was not unthinkable for first-century Jews to suppose that, within the mystery of the One God, there might be different movements, different energies, contributing together to the work of creation and new creation. The first followers of Jesus were saying something like that about him and about his Spirit. This then joins up with our earlier discussions of the Trinity and of Jesus's messiahship.

From our point of view this may seem quite complicated. But did we really think that trying to understand the greatest mystery of all would be straightforward? For John the simplicity we all crave is found in the compelling and deeply human portrait of Jesus himself. Look at him, says John, and whatever you thought you knew about God before, rethink it with him in the middle of it all. "Nobody has ever seen God. The only-begotten God, who is intimately close to the father—he has brought him to light" (1:18). That says it all.

Chapter Seven

Power

SOME YEARS AGO I WROTE A BOOK ABOUT POWER. IT WAS about God's kingdom, which, according to one of Jesus's striking predictions in the gospels, will "come in power" (Mark 9:1). That, of course, was what his contemporaries were longing for. God would do at last what he had promised in the scriptures and take over the running of this world in a whole new way. So my book, *How God Became King*, tried to explain that the announcement of God's kingdom by Jesus and then later by the early Christian community was basically all about God's taking charge and running the world in a whole new way.

Among the puzzled letters and emails I received from people who read the book was one that put the problem quite starkly. So, said my correspondent, imagine there is a great crisis: a nuclear attack, a global pandemic, or a massive natural disaster. Someone goes to the prime minister, the president, or whoever is supposed to be running the country and says, "What are you going to do about this?" and back comes the answer, "It's all right—you see, God's in charge now."

The point was obvious. If God's in charge, the rest of us can sit back and wait for God to act in whatever way is best—and we might be waiting a long time. In other words, my correspondent was saying, that's just not good enough. Something needs to be done. By us.

This is our modern version of a very old debate. One of the things that divided Jewish thinkers in Jesus's day was the question of whether they should wait passively (albeit prayerfully) for God to act (the Essenes more or less believed that), whether they should get on and run things themselves and assume that God would bless it (the Sadducees), or whether there should be a mixture of human initiative and divine action (the Pharisees, with further differences between them). There was also the house of Herod, the nominal "kings of the Jews," who don't seem to have bothered too much about God as long as they could stay in power themselves—which meant doing deals with the biggest power of the day, namely, Caesar in Rome.

We have our own versions of the same dilemma. And this brings into focus the problem of power—which has the same shape as the other six problems we have looked at in this book. One could state it simply: *we all know power matters, but we all know it can easily go badly wrong.*

Of course, many people in our day have come to see "power" as a dirty word. I have often enough heard people say, during discussions in churches, businesses, and universities, "Oh, it's all about power." In other words, the discussion is supposed to be about a matter of policy, but what's really going on is that different groups are jockeying for power and using this issue as a way of grabbing it, and we think the whole thing stinks. It can get worse: people who say, "It's all about power," can themselves be accused of wanting power and simply resenting the fact that the other side seems to be winning. Accusing people of trying to grab at power can itself constitute a power grab.

But can we do without power? Clearly not. Things have to be done. Laws have to be made and (more or less) enforced. Infrastructure—roads, phone systems, electricity supplies, and so on—have to be maintained. The trains have to run—if not precisely on time ("making the trains run on time" has become a cliché for the workings of tyrannical regimes like that of Nazi Germany), then at least fairly reliably, so people can get to work and home again. We might occasionally fantasize about doing without power altogether and living a "simple" life, dependent on no one but ourselves, but those who have attempted such a desert-island lifestyle have found it challenging, to say the least. Even a nuclear family on a remote island will need someone in charge. Several of our other major themes—justice, relationships, and so on—presuppose at least a basic community in which decisions have to be made and implemented. And that means power.

Plenty of people down through the years have approached things from the other end and declared that the way to get things done is to put a strong man (it's usually a man) in charge. People have then made distinctions between "monarchy" (rule by a king or perhaps queen, surrounded by advisers and authorized administrators) and "tyranny" (rule by one all-powerful person who makes all decisions totally at will and implements them, often with force). Sometimes tyranny is shared by a small group, for which the technical term used to be "oligarchy"—though today that word means something different.

So the debate goes back and forth, at national and international levels and in schools, colleges, businesses, and families. Those who have suffered under bullying tyrants sometimes appear to favor anarchy instead; they reason that if people are allowed to do whatever they want, it will remove the temptation for the arrogant and powerful to crush everybody else! But that regularly has the opposite effect.

We saw that in Iraq in 2003 and 2004. Saddam Hussein had been given more power than was wise, because the Western allies had wanted Iraq as a buffer state against Iran when that country became a theocratic Islamic state in 1979. But when Saddam himself became a ruthless, murderous tyrant, the Western powers decided to overthrow him, supposing naively that once he was gone, peace, happiness, and Western-style democracy would spring up automatically. Instead, as we know, there was anarchy—which, predictably, enabled the bullies and the unscrupulous to do whatever they wanted. In fact, the poor and the weak were marginally better protected under the old tyranny than under the subsequent anarchy, whose effects are still being felt throughout the region.

There, then, is the dilemma. Lord Acton, a nineteenth-century British historian, is regularly quoted: "Power tends to corrupt," he said, "and absolute power corrupts absolutely." Yes, indeed. But Lord Acton was not so clear on what should be done to prevent the corruption that so easily creeps in. The story of global politics in general and of politics in the Western world in particular over the last 250 years has been the story of different attempts to answer that question. We have seen revolutions, the extension of democratic franchise, socialist governments, right-wing dictatorships, and various kinds of compromises and coalitions.

Some suggest that different types of government suit different cultures and ethnic groups; others suspect that proposal of closet racism. Meanwhile, often, led as we are by the media, we mock weak leaders, but resent powerful ones. We want justice (as we saw earlier), and if justice is to flourish, there must be some kind of power. But, as we know, people in power regularly bend justice to suit their own ends, to avoid having their corrupt behavior come to light, and to use the full force of the law against their opponents. Power is a problem at the global and international level.

You see the same thing even more sharply in schools, businesses, churches, and families. Things go well when there's a strong, clear lead "from the top," as we say—until the person "at the top" forgets that the locomotive leading the train has to remain attached to the cars. Some leaders, all too aware of this, stop leading and simply try to "manage," but that's disastrous as well. If the driver isn't holding the steering wheel, either the truck will careen wildly, uncontrolled, across the road, or everybody else in the truck will try to grab it. Neither way ends well.

Thus both extremes—the abuse of power and the abdication of it—point to the ongoing dilemma of power itself. Two or three generations ago the pendulum was swinging toward "strong" central control, whether of the Soviet kind or the Nazi kind. Many "liberal" thinkers in the 1920s and 1930s, tired of the stupidity of democratic governments, assumed that Russia and Germany were leading the way and that the rest of us were bound to follow. The bad memories of those days still hang like a dark cloud on our recent historical horizon, and the mood has swung back toward an abiding suspicion of "institutions" and the power they wield—or that people imagine they wield. "The system" and "the establishment" have become terms of abuse almost as much as "power" itself.

This protest—associated with the loose movement known as postmodernism—has been applied across the board. If someone says they are acting out of love, we suspect it's really a power play. If someone offers you "freedom," you *know* it's a power play. And when someone says they are telling you "the honest truth," we are uncomfortably aware that, like Pilate, what they almost certainly mean is that they, being in power, are creating a "truth" to make the world the way they want it and to retain their power. And so it goes.

All this brings us, once more, to the climax of John's gospel. With Pilate and Jesus confronting one another, we discover that the entire story has been about power—about what it really is, how it really works, and the radically different sort of power the gospel displays. Power, in other words, is the final broken signpost. It appears to tell us something vital about the world, and perhaps also about the world's creator. But, again and again, it lets us down so badly that we easily become cynical and want to say that the whole thing is just a nightmare or a joke in bad taste.

John's story of Jesus gives a very different answer. Power does indeed matter. It is indeed a signpost to the reality of the true God. But true power is very different from what most people expect or assume it to be.

Before we can dive into John's gospel, however, we need to

look at the backstory from Israel's scriptures. John, and Jesus before him, could assume it; people today, including many Christians, have all but forgotten it.

Power and the Human Vocation

Human beings are given power on the very first page of the Bible. In Genesis 1, various features of the newly made world (vegetation, birds, and animals) are given instructions to multiply, to flourish, to get on with being themselves and with propagating their own species. When humans are made, however, there is an extra dimension. Humans too are commanded to be fruitful and multiply (1:28), but they are given an extra awesome and responsible vocation: to "have dominion over the fish of the sea, over the birds of the air, and over the cattle, and over all the wild animals of the earth, and over every creeping thing that creeps upon the earth" (1:26, 28). Power, in other words, comes from God and is given to human beings.

Howls of protest have greeted this kind of statement, as you'd expect, granted the social mood I described a moment ago. We are only too well aware of the destructive results when people hear the word "dominion" and assume that it means "exploitation." Some have seen this as the root cause of our present environmental crisis. Some have urged that we regard this vocation as cancelled by the "fall" in Genesis 3, but we find it again in Psalm 8, which the early Christians regularly cited in connection with Jesus himself.

In that poem, celebrating the greatness and majesty of God

himself, the Psalmist declares that, although humans are apparently small and insignificant compared with the sun, moon, and stars, God has "crowned them with glory and honor," giving them "dominion" (that word again) over the rest of the earth. I do not think the Psalmist was naive. The dangerous folly of the human race was all too apparent then as now. But the vocation is reaffirmed—setting up the biblical version of the puzzle we have already sketched. How does the Bible itself resolve it?

One of the principal ways in which the issue is resolved in the Bible Jesus knew is through the theme of wisdom. Human beings are called to be "wise," to find that, through humble reverence before the living creator God, they themselves will gain insight and understanding into how to manage not only their own lives, but all the other aspects of the world in which they find themselves. The classic text here is the book of Proverbs and the various other Jewish texts that expound and apply it. In particular, the vocation to be the chief ruler of God's people was seen to require "wisdom" of a type that could only be the gift of God. Solomon, aware of his awesome responsibilities, prays for wisdom, so that he can rule as king with proper discernment between good and evil (1 Kings 3:6–9).

This theme is developed in two famous portraits of biblical heroes who, without becoming kings as such, are acknowledged by the actual rulers to possess superior wisdom and are therefore put in authority under the king and over the kingdom, much the way humans are under God and over the world. The two are Joseph in the court of Pharaoh and Daniel in the court at Babylon. Their stories display the nuanced ways in which their power was rooted in faithfulness to God, expressed in remarkable insight, recognized by their respective monarchs, and exercised in practice.

When it comes to kings themselves, another psalm holds out a majestic vision of the ways in which "dominion" is supposed to be exercised:

> Give the king your justice, O God,
> and your righteousness to a king's son.
> May he judge your people with righteousness,
> and your poor with justice. . . .
> May he have dominion from sea to sea,
> and from the River to the ends of the earth. . . .
> For he delivers the needy when they call,
> the poor and those who have no helper.
> He has pity on the weak and the needy,
> and saves the lives of the needy.
> From oppression and violence he redeems their life;
> and precious is their blood in his sight. (72:1–2, 8, 12–14)

That's what "dominion" is there for. It can easily be exploited for one's own advantage, as we all know. The stories of monarchies, including the ancient Hebrew monarchies, are full of such abuses, but there is a true use to which rulers can and must be recalled. God wants his world to be ruled wisely, by humble and obedient humans in every sphere, by people who will rely on God's own judgment and wisdom and who will implement it in their communities to bring healing and hope to those most in need of it. The psalm ends with the ultimate promise: under the rule of such a king, God's glory will fill the whole earth (72:19).

This vision of God's chosen king as the wise, healing ruler is then held up for the rulers of the other nations to see and be humbled. "Now therefore, O kings, be wise," writes the Psalmist; "be warned, O rulers of the earth" (2:10). This theme echoes down through the centuries and is picked up in the much later book known as the Wisdom of Solomon (6:1).

The instinct for suspecting all rulers of corruption and self-seeking was of course fully recognized in the ancient Israelite and then Jewish communities. The checks and balances that power requires were supplied through the strange and often danger-ous vocation of the prophets. They too needed wisdom; they too were susceptible to corruption and deceit. When a bad king seeks advice from a false prophet, the people should tremble (as we see, for instance, in 1 Kings 22). But as a general rule it was recognized that kings and priests (priests exercised their own kind of authority) needed to be held to account and that proph-ets were the people to do it. That was why the Second Temple period of Jewish life must have been so confusing to those who were prayerfully struggling to cling on to faith and hope. The ancient royal house had failed. The priests were corrupt. No prophets arose to tell people what was going on.

And this was why, when there appeared a man who answered to the description of "prophet," denouncing the present "king of the Jews" and declaring that any minute now the true king would be revealed, there was enormous excitement. Now at last, peo-ple believed, God would "take charge," would "become king," in the way some had always wanted. And when this prophet's cousin, Jesus of Nazareth, began to perform powerful deeds and declare that God's kingdom was indeed being launched, the ex-citement overflowed. People in power took note. They watched with care and, we may assume, a measure of alarm.

Like our other main signposts, then, the theme of power can bring us back quite quickly to Jesus himself. In this case, in

fact, to Jesus precisely as a true human being. When people ex-
claim that Jesus was acting with great power and authority, we
shouldn't short-circuit the process and assume that this means
he was simply "being God," but rather that he was being the
ultimately obedient human being, the true king, the one put
in authority over the world. Jesus's power was used precisely as
Psalm 72 said it should be. It forms the model for all genuine
human power.

The long and often puzzling story of Israel thus reaches its
climax (this is what all four gospels are trying to tell us) in
the life of this one man. But not just in his life. Jesus himself
explicitly redefined power in a famous passage, and he did so
around his own vocation-within-a-vocation. He would bring
the Genesis-based human vocation (to "dominion") and the
royal vocation (to "healing power") to their climax through
his own death:

> James and John, Zebedee's sons, came up to him.
>
> "Teacher," they said, "we want you to grant us
> whatever we ask."
>
> "What do you want me to do for you?" asked Jesus.
>
> "Grant us," they said, "that when you're there in all
> your glory, one of us will sit at your right, and the other at
> your left."
>
> "You don't know what you're asking for!" Jesus replied.
> "Can you drink the cup I'm going to drink? Can you
> receive the baptism I'm going to receive?"
>
> "Yes," they said, "we can."
>
> "Well," said Jesus, "you will drink the cup I drink;
> you will receive the baptism I receive. But sitting at my

right hand or my left—that's not up to me. It's been assigned already."

When the other ten disciples heard, they were angry with James and John. Jesus called them to him.

"You know how it is in the pagan nations," he said. "Think how their so-called rulers act. They lord it over their subjects. The high and mighty ones boss the rest around. But that's not how it's going to be with you. Anyone who wants to be great among you must become your servant. Anyone who wants to be first must be everyone's slave. Don't you see? The son of man didn't come to be waited on. He came to be the servant, to give his life 'as a ransom for many.'" (Mark 10:35–45)

This is one of several major passages in the New Testament that offers this kind of redefinition of power. The fact that many have preached on this text without noticing that this is what it's all about—instead focusing solely on the very last sentence and treating it as a detached statement of "atonement theology"—is a symptom of the deep malaise that has gripped so much of Western Christianity, a "spiritualization" of the faith that makes it only about "me and my salvation" and not at all about the real world. This in turn explains why many have supposed that the Bible has nothing much to say about the great issues of our day, of which power is undoubtedly one.

But the passage as a whole is very clear. Jesus is simultaneously affirming the God-given nature of power, challenging the regular corruption of it, particularly among kings and emperors, and redefining it around his own scripture-based vocation. The sovereign rule of God that he was inaugurating in his public

career would be firmly established not through the kind of revolution that James and John had in mind, but through his own
scripture-fulfilling death.

That is one of the key biblical passages about power; another
is Paul's Second Letter to the Corinthians. Without going into
detail, suffice it to say that one of the underlying themes in that
complicated and challenging letter is Paul's confrontation with
those in Corinth who wanted, as it were, to "make apostle-
ship great again." He disagrees and sets them straight. Although
being an apostle of Jesus the crucified Messiah does indeed carry
power—and power is necessary if the church is not to collapse
back into anarchic paganism—the power in question is that
shown by the Messiah himself through his death and resurrection. "When I'm weak," he insists, "then I am strong" (12:10).

The whole letter forms an extended meditation on that theme,
applied with great subtlety and pathos. I suspect that many in our
churches, including many who think of themselves as "Pauline"
Christians, are comparatively unfamiliar with Second Corinthians, perhaps again because the Western church does not expect to
learn about power from studying the Bible. But it's time we did.

The initial biblical answer to the question about power, then,
is that power undoubtedly has an important place within the
Creator's purpose for the world, but that (like justice, freedom,
and all the rest) it can be, and regularly is, corrupted in ways that
seem to undermine any chance of its being a signpost to ultimate truth about God and the world. But in fact power really is
a signpost of that kind, since it points to the fact that the Creator
intended, and still intends, that his world should be ordered, not
chaotic; fruitful, not wasteful; glorifying to him, rather than
shameful. And the central design the creator God has put in

place to accomplish this is his delegation of his power to his image-bearing human creatures.

God is quite capable, of course, of acting directly in the world, though even then the Bible often reckons with humans being taken up into this work as well, if only by their lament and intercession. But there are several hints in scripture that the design of creation itself—a world made by God to blossom and flourish under human stewardship—was a reflection of the secret, hidden truth about the Creator himself. God, it seems, made a world designed to work through human agency, against the day when he would come as a genuine human to take charge of his world himself. Much theology of the last three hundred years has struggled to emphasize the divinity of Jesus and hasn't been sure what to do with his humanity or with the question of how they might actually work together. This is the answer, at least in principle—and, with this, the answer as well to our question about power:

> He is the image of God, the invisible one,
> The firstborn of all creation.
> For in him all things were created,
> In the heavens and here on the earth.
> Things we can see and things we cannot—
> Thrones and lordships and rulers and powers—
> All things were created both through him and for him.
>   (Col. 1:15–16)

"He is the image"; that is, he is the genuine human being, and also, a few verses later, the one in whom all God's fullness was glad to dwell (1:19). As Paul explains in the next chapter,

"In him all the full measure of divinity has taken up bodily residence" (2:9). All power, then, belongs to God and is delegated to the Son—who then delegates it further, to the "thrones, lordships, rulers, and powers" of this world. This is a challenging statement in our present political climate, where suspicion and anti-authoritarian rhetoric have become the unthinking order of the day. But Paul (writing this letter from prison!) is neither naive nor idealistic. Indeed, he says that God had "stripped the rulers and authorities of their armor, and displayed them contemptuously to public view, celebrating his triumph over them in him" [that is, in Jesus] (2:15). If the "powers" were made in, through, and for the Son, they seem to have rebelled. They needed to be defeated and brought back into line. But when that happens, they are not abolished; they are "reconciled" (1:20).

I think we can go a step further. It isn't just that God has created a world in which humans are called to exercise delegated authority. It isn't just that this seems to be because God always intended to come and exercise this power himself, in and as a human being. It is also the case that this power sharing, this delegation to a creature that by itself is weak, vulnerable, prey to sickness and attack by wild beasts, and limited in knowledge and physical power, speaks volumes about the Creator's generous, overflowing love.

How easy it has been, when people have glimpsed the human vocation to exercise this God-given power in the world, for them to "play God"—while forgetting that the God they ought to be imitating is not the God of naked, bullying power, but the God of generous, outgoing love, the power-sharing God, the God who works through vulnerable humans, the God who came and exercised his saving power as an utterly vulnerable human, "a man of sorrows, and acquainted with grief," as the King James Version translates Isaiah 53:3.

One might even say that the abuse of power, which has caused so many in our day to regard power itself not as a signpost to the truth about God and the world but as an unpleasant and regrettable feature of the way the world really is (and perhaps even as an argument against the existence of God!), goes hand in hand with a failure in the Western church and world to understand the doctrine of the Trinity itself. It is through the mysterious truth that God the Creator always intended to come into his creation in and as a human being that we can ultimately understand what power is all about.

When, with the world in ruins, that entry of God-as-human into the world necessitated the most dramatic inversion imaginable of the normal concepts of power—Jesus coming into his kingdom through the shameful torture of the cross—we begin to glimpse that part of our problem with theology itself is that we have projected back onto God the various images of power we have gleaned from its abuse, rather than allowing the vision of God displayed in the gospels to reorient and realign all that we might want to say about God in the first place. The whole New Testament insists that we only know who God really is—and, with that, that we only know what power really is—by looking at Jesus himself.

When Paul spoke of his own power as an apostle, the power of the Spirit at work in and through him, he insisted that this power too was displayed in and through his apparently shameful weakness. If it is true, as we are told in various places, that God's ultimate plan is to make redeemed humans his "royal priesthood" in the eventual new creation (Rev. 1:6; 5:10; and elsewhere), this delegated stewardship will itself be a matter of redefined power, the power of sovereign, self-giving love. The more we anticipate this kind of power in the present, the better—not least because the broken signpost of power as we presently know it might find itself being mended at last.

The Two Kinds of Power

Back to John's gospel. What does John say about power?

The primary answer is found in the confrontation between Jesus and Pilate in chapters 18–19. This is, of course, anything but a meeting of equals. The onlookers see a lonely, defenseless man whose own countrymen want him killed; a vulnerable man, flogged on the whim of the governor, sneered at by soldiers who dress him up as a fake "king"; a helpless man, entirely at the mercy of the power of the day. John's readers, though, see the Word made flesh, the Lord of Creation, the King of Israel, and hence (according to the Psalms and the Prophets) the true Lord of the world.

The onlookers see a Roman governor who is able to kill one man and release another as he pleases—though, eventually, he is answerable to Caesar, who may not take too kindly to the thought that a rebel "king" has been let off lightly ("If you let this fellow go," shouted the Judaean leaders, "you are no friend of Caesar!" 19:12). John's readers see a weak politician, in over his head, angry at being manipulated, determined to get his petty revenge ("What I've written, I've written," v. 22). In particular, they see in Pilate what Jesus saw: a human being with genuine delegated authority ("You couldn't have any authority at all over me unless it was given to you from above," v. 11) and who will therefore be held responsible for what he does with it, a responsibility belonging even more squarely to those who have handed Jesus over to him ("That's why the person who handed me over to you is guilty of a greater sin," v. 11).

Even at this moment of crisis, the ancient biblical understanding of political power, especially pagan political power, holds firm: the One God wants his world to be governed wisely by human beings—and those to whom this authority is delegated will be held to account. Tyrants love the first part of that sentence and try to forget the second. Those who prefer anarchy stress the second part and try to forget the first.

What this is all about, from Jesus's and John's point of view, is the kingdom of God. "Kingdom" is about authority, and authority is ultimately about power. But supposing there are different kinds of power? As always, even at a moment like this, Jesus answers the question his interlocutors should have asked rather than the one they actually asked:

> So Pilate went back in to the Praetorium and spoke to Jesus.
>
> "Are you the king of the Jews?" he asked.
>
> "Was it *your* idea to ask that?" asked Jesus. "Or did other people tell you about me?"
>
> "I'm not a Jew, am I?" retorted Pilate. "Your own people, and the chief priests, have handed you over to me! What have you done?"
>
> "My kingdom isn't the sort that grows in this world," replied Jesus. "If my kingdom were from this world, my supporters would have fought to stop me being handed

over to the Judaeans. So, then, my kingdom is not the sort that comes from here." (18:33–36)

The crucial sentence is this one: *My kingdom isn't the sort that grows in this world.* There are two kinds of kingdoms, two kinds of power. Older translations such as the King James Version often gave people the wrong idea in rendering the sentence as, "My kingdom is not of this world." In a culture that positively wants the message of Jesus to have nothing to do with "power" at all, that sounds as though he were saying, "My kingdom is all about going to heaven"—so please don't bother about anything "worldly" at all.

But that's not what the sentence says in the original language. Jesus's kingdom is not "from this world," but it is certainly *for* this world. This is the direct application of the line in the Lord's Prayer that says, "Thy kingdom come on earth as in heaven." The kingdom comes from heaven, but it is designed to take effect on earth. It is designed, in fact, to be the true sort of kingly power, the sort that Psalm 72 was talking about, the sort that is truly a signpost to the reality of God and the truth about the world, however much that signpost has been damaged along the way.

So what is the crucial difference between the two sorts of kingdoms, the two kinds of power? Jesus is quite explicit. A "worldly" kingdom, in the sense he is rejecting, makes its way as worldly kingdoms do—through fighting. That is how Caesar's kingdom worked, with ruthless efficiency. If Jesus's kingdom was "from this world," his followers and supporters would have staged an armed rebellion. Actually—and John's original readers knew this only too well—that might quite easily have happened when Simon Peter drew his sword in the garden and cut off the ear of the high priest's servant, Malchus (18:10).

That moment, heightened by the fact that John knows the servant's name and highlights it, sharpens the contrast between the two kinds of kingdom, the two kinds of power, and shows that even Jesus's closest supporters, having heard all that he had said about the powerful love of God, still hadn't "gotten it." Love might be all right when Jesus and his followers were sitting around the table together, but when there was business to be done in the outside world, then presumably one would need a sword, as one always did. Not so, declares Jesus. This dialogue too—just like Jesus's confrontation with Pilate—is still held under the rubric of John 13:1: this entire story is about love itself, Love in the flesh, doing what only love can do.

One might indeed turn to that chapter, John 13, for further expansion of the same point. In v. 3 John says, "Jesus knew that the father had given everything into his hands." God had delegated to him the task of bringing in the kingdom. And the way he chooses to express that power, that authority, is by kneeling down to wash the disciples' feet (vv. 4–15), insisting that this is to serve as the model for how his followers are to act thereafter. This, we might suggest, is part of what is in view when, at the heart of the gospel's prologue, John says that "to anyone who did accept him he gave the right"—the Greek is *exousia*, the "power" or "authority"—"to become God's children" (1:12). Children are not usually reckoned among the powerful of the world. What it means to be a child of God is then defined by the rest of the story, particularly the foot washing, on the one hand, and the crucifixion, on the other.

The foregoing points need now to be grounded more clearly

in the analysis of power and victory in chapter 12. If we want to know what John thought was happening when Jesus was confronting Pilate—and when Pilate was exercising the "normal" sort of kingdom by sending Jesus to his death—we need to pay close attention to 12:20–33:

> Some Greeks had come up with all the others to worship at the festival. They went to Philip, who was from Bethsaida in Galilee.
>
> "Sir," they said, "we would like to see Jesus."
>
> Philip went and told Andrew, and Andrew and Philip went together to tell Jesus.
>
> "The time has come," said Jesus in reply. "This is the moment for the son of man to be glorified. I'm telling you the solemn truth: unless a grain of wheat falls into the earth and dies, it remains all by itself. If it dies, though, it will produce lots of fruit. If you love your life, you'll lose it. If you hate your life in this world, you'll keep it for the life of the coming age.
>
> "If anyone serves me, they must follow me. Where I am, my servant will be too. If anyone serves me, the father will honor them."
>
> "Now my heart is troubled," Jesus went on. "What am I going to say—'Father, save me from this moment?' No! It was because of this that I came to this moment. Father, glorify your name!"
>
> "I have glorified it," came a voice from heaven, "and I will glorify it again."
>
> "That was thunder!" said the crowd, standing there listening.

"No," said others. "It was an angel, talking to him."

"That voice came for your sake, not mine," replied Jesus. "Now comes the judgment of this world! Now this world's ruler is going to be thrown out! And when I've been lifted up from the earth, I will draw all people to myself."

He said this in order to point to the kind of death he was going to die.

The underlying question here—and John, we remember, is good at underlying questions!—is: Who is really in charge of the world? This is the question of the kingdom; the question, too, of justice, as we saw in our first chapter. But now it is approached from what seems to us to be an oblique angle.

The passage starts in quite a low-key, friendly way. Jesus and his followers are in Jerusalem, and, not surprisingly, word has gotten around. Pilgrims who have come from near and far are eager to experience all that Jerusalem has to offer. Jesus has become, for a brief moment, almost a tourist attraction. We might expect that he would be happy to talk to the Greeks, to explain to them something about the true kingdom of the true God.

But as usual John confounds our expectations, just as Jesus himself had done. Instead of grasping what looks to us like "an evangelistic opportunity," Jesus interprets the approach of the Greeks as a sign that the end game is rapidly approaching. "This is the moment for the son of man to be glorified," he says—in other words, for Daniel 7 to come true at last and for "one like a son of man," the royal representative of Israel, to assume his proper authority over the world. Jesus sees that this is the moment for the real transfer of power to take place.

But this transfer of power will not be achieved through the normal means, the means that Peter was grasping for in his disastrous moment in the garden. It will be accomplished by "a grain of wheat falling into the earth and dying," and so bearing "lots of fruit." Jesus must win the victory by this totally unexpected route, and his followers must in turn learn that same kingdom behavior. This is how the Father's glory will be unveiled. The Father has glorified his name and will do so once more, decisively. Jesus interprets the voice from heaven as the sign of imminent victory: "Now comes the judgment of this world! Now this world's ruler is going to be thrown out! And when I've been lifted up from the earth, I will draw all people to myself."

This, in other words, is the oblique answer to the request from the Greeks. Yes, their request is a sign that the last act of the drama is fast approaching. The "son of man" is going to be exalted as the Lord of the Nations, to draw "all people" to himself. But for this to happen, the one who currently wields the power must be overthrown. The world itself is being held to account ("judged"), and the world's ruler, who at present has power over the whole world including the Greeks, is going to be dethroned. This incident, we remind ourselves, comes near the dramatic conclusion of the first half of John's book, indicating to us how the second half is then to be read.

When, at the climax of that second half, we see Jesus confronting Pontius Pilate, this is what is going on. This is how "the ruler" is being judged, held to account, shown up as being in league with the ultimate anticreation force. This is the model for the agenda Jesus has set the church in chapter 16; this is what it will look like when, through the church's witness, the Spirit will "prove the world to be in the wrong" about sin, justice, and judgment (16:8–11). John's readers have already been told that victory over "the world's ruler" will come through Jesus's death. That will then be implemented through the work of the Spirit, "proving the world to be in the wrong," and through the gospel, drawing people from every nation into the new family of Jesus.

The phrase "the world's ruler" seems therefore to have two meanings here in chapter 12. We find it difficult to hold these meanings together; other cultures have sometimes found it easier than we do. At one level, there is no question who is being spoken of. This "world ruler" is the dark power, the power of "the satan," the accuser. "The satan" will shortly be putting ideas into Judas's heart and will then actually enter that heart, directing it, so that Judas actually becomes "the accuser" who leads the soldiers to arrest Jesus (13:2, 27). This "ruler of the world" is going to do the worst—and will discover, in having Jesus killed, that his death is actually the means of the victory Jesus had predicted.

But at the same time it seems clear that "the world's ruler" is also the force of Rome, of Caesar. Jesus declares a little later that "the ruler of the world is coming" (14:30). Even though this "ruler" has, as Jesus says, "nothing to do with me," he will for a moment appear to have gotten Jesus in his power. This time it is clear that Jesus is talking about the soldiers who will arrest him and finally crucify him. Somehow the two referents of "the world's ruler" run together. "The satan" and the soldiers will be working hand in glove. And all this will be simply the means to the end, the victory planned by the Father.

When we then put together John 12 with John 18–19, we

discover that John has woven what he wants to say about power, about the kingdom of God itself, into the larger narrative. If Jesus's kingdom were "from this world," his servants would fight. Pilate has that kind of authority too, the authority to have Jesus killed. This is "normal" power, the usual method of "kingdom." But Jesus's kind of power works the other way. It works through suffering love, through the one who gives his life for his friends, the one who is lifted up like the serpent in the wilderness so that all may see him, believe, and be rescued—rescued from the grip of the other power, the dark power. And the ultimate rescue from the ultimate dark power is of course resurrection.

Thus, when Lazarus turned out to be still incorrupt after four days in the tomb and was apparently waiting for Jesus's command to wake him from death, this was the sign to Jesus that his earlier prayers had been answered. When Jesus himself was raised from the dead on the third day, this was the sign that the work of ultimate rescue had indeed been "accomplished," "finished," when he died on the cross (19:30). Easter declares, in power (that is part of the point, as Paul sees it in Rom. 1:3–4), that "the ruler of this world" has indeed been "cast out"—and that now is the time for the Greeks, and anyone else who wants to, to leave their worthless idols and worship the true God.

Ordinary power and the ordinary kingdoms of the world have death as their ultimate weapon. God's kingdom and the power that goes with it can overcome death. The Creator's power renews creation itself. The resurrection is the ultimate answer to Pilate's questions and, with them, to the problem of power itself.

The Power of the Spirit in the Present

At this point someone might object: "Well, supposing there is going to be a resurrection at the end, when everything will be put right; what about in the interim before then? Surely we have to go on using the normal means of power, power with the ultimate threat of enforcement, violence, and death itself up to that point, right?"

Well, here we have to be careful. There is a biblical view according to which, in the present time, all societies still need police work to prevent the bullies and the unscrupulous from preying on the weak and vulnerable. That is what Paul is talking about in Romans 13:1–7, and Peter in 1 Peter 2:13–17. But that is simply the sign that the final kingdom, at the return of Jesus himself (as in, e.g., John 21:22 or Phil. 3:20–21), has not yet taken place. This kind of police action has a strictly limited purpose. It is rather like the role of Torah as explained by Paul in Galatians 3: to keep evil in check until the Messiah comes. So "police" work of the Romans 13 variety is necessary to prevent anarchy and chaos in the world until the Messiah returns. But that kind of work is not the means by which the kingdom of God itself, launched decisively in Jesus's death and resurrection, goes forward in the present time.

That work is accomplished, John insists, through the power of the Spirit. Now that the dark power has been defeated; now that Jesus's followers have been made clean by his word and by his death; now that Jesus has been "glorified," "lifted up" on the cross, and raised to new, immortal bodily life—Jesus's followers are to be equipped with his Spirit, breathed on them after the resurrection, so that they can obey his command, "As the

father has sent me, so I'm sending you" (20:21). And they go to
their tasks, like travelers entering a strange, unmapped new land,
without the trappings of the "kingdoms" and the "powers" that
are "from this world," but with the world-changing, people-
changing power of the gospel and the Spirit.

This means that Jesus's followers, empowered by the Spirit, are
themselves taking on the role of the truly human beings, exercising the truly human power. Jesus was the truly human one,
the image-bearer, the one who completed the story of the "new
Genesis." When he comes out before the crowds, clothed ironically in the purple robe, Pilate says more than he knows: "Look!
Here's the man!" (19:5). Here, just as when Pilate calls Jesus "king
of the Jews," John is clear that he is speaking the truth, even
though he means it cynically. Jesus is the true Man, the Image,
the King—and his followers, the branches of the true vine, those
who share his body and blood and are indwelt and empowered by
his Spirit, are themselves the truly human ones.

Here at last we have the answer to the paradox of power. Humans are made to exercise power, but true human power was
always intended to be exercised through self-giving love. When
that happens, power "works." It may not always achieve the instant "results" obtained by threats, bullying, and violence. But
that's part of the point—and it's part of the reason why, against
the sneer of today's Pontius Pilates, God's kingdom is not roll-
ing out smoothly the way some might like. Rather, it makes its
way as it always did, through the suffering witness of Christian
outcasts, through the Mother Teresas of this world, through the
self-giving love of "ordinary" Jesus followers, through the shout
of "Jesus!" that was heard in 2015 from those Coptic Christians
beheaded on a beach in Libya.

That, indeed, is what John 21 is all about. This chapter, which seems to have been added after the death of the original author by someone close to him who could vouch for his stories, highlights the moment when Peter, after his earlier disastrous lapse, is recommissioned to be a leader among Jesus's followers. Two things emerge here about the nature of power.

First, the authority Peter will gain through this recommissioning comes when he is fully aware of his weakness and failure. Much ordinary human "power" is sustained through the pretense of all-conquering strength. Peter's, symbolizing here the true power of those who bring the gospel to the world, remains a gift from Jesus precisely to those who know that they are both unworthy and incapable. The minute they forget that, they are heading for trouble. The later stories about Peter's own crucifixion—and his insisting that he be crucified upside down so as not to be compared with Jesus himself—may not be well founded historically. But they show how subsequent generations had been gripped with this vision of ordinary power being subverted in the lives of Jesus's followers.

Second, the power and authority now vested in Peter are not at all like the kind of power he himself had wanted to wield when he drew his sword in the garden. That, indeed, was the real sign of his failure. Having imagined that Jesus could be defended by ordinary, old-fashioned human violence, he then had nowhere to hide when he was himself confronted with even the hint of a threat ("Didn't I see you in the garden with him?"). Rather, the power and authority he will now have is likened to looking after a flock of sheep: "Feed my lambs. Look after my sheep. Feed my sheep." The lambs and sheep are the ones that matter. The shepherd simply has a job to do. It is, to be sure, a commission that carries power, but it consists wholly of the work of love.

In the end, then, the Christian message offers a profound reversal of what we think we know about power, and indeed what we want from it. When we follow the trail of the broken signposts, we find that they lead us to the foot of the cross, where our anxious questions are finally resolved. The kingdoms of the world insist that power must be achieved and sustained by the threat of violence. That is why power has become such a paradox: it seems to begin as a signpost to the truth of the world, but it points in directions that make most of us shudder.

Rather, God's kingdom reveals something quite different—a power exercised through giving, serving, and loving. A power that transforms the world in ways nobody could imagine at the time, in ways that today's anxious secularists do their best to hush up. A power that calls, confronts, transforms, and then equips more and more people from every conceivable background to be in their turn powerful witnesses to the Jesus they have come to know and love. The gospel message insists that the signpost we saw as broken was indeed a true pointer to the ultimate reality of God and the world. But, as with the other six, we could only discern its meaning when we approached it in light of the story of Jesus and his death.

Conclusion

Mending the Broken Signposts

I T'S TIME TO DRAW THE THREADS OF OUR DISCUSSION TO-
gether. Let me summarize where I think we've come to.

I described the seven themes of justice, love, spirituality, beauty, freedom, truth, and power as "broken signposts." By this I mean two things. First, the universal human longings for these things are all genuine signposts to the fact that we humans are made by a good and wise Creator. Especially when you put all seven together, this makes—at one level!—a whole lot of sense.

But, second, given the way things currently are, we find that each one of them is "broken." They fail to deliver on what they appear to promise. Or perhaps we should say, *we* fail to deliver. We know that justice, freedom, truth, and the rest matter very much, but we conveniently ignore them when it suits us, and we seem to be very bad at setting up systems to make them happen. As a result, it's quite possible for people to look at these various human longings and aspirations and to draw all sorts of different conclusions, one of which would be that they are merely accidental evolutionary developments and have no meaning whatever beyond that.

But the way in which each of the signposts "fails"—justice denied, love trampled upon, power abused, and so on—corresponds in an almost eerie fashion to the way in which, in all four gospels and particularly John's majestic account, Jesus of Nazareth went to his death, with a kangaroo trial, friends betraying and denying him, truth sneered at, and all the rest. And this, I have suggested, is the reason why Jesus's crucifixion still functions, across different human cultures and not least in our own apparently "secular" world, as a sign of hope, a strange pointer to a God who is radically different from all other "gods." Jesus's crucifixion resonates with the broken signposts of which all humans are at least dimly aware. Indeed, the cross, with all the irony and horror that attaches to it, is to be seen itself as the ultimate broken signpost.

What follows from this? I have argued that for these signposts now to "work" as outward-facing signs of the presence and reality of the true God—to communicate that reality, presence, and indeed love to those presently without faith—it is vital that the followers of Jesus use those signposts to frame their vocations. When those who seek to tell others about the God of creation and new creation and about his sending his Son to enact his rescuing love are working in their communities on projects demonstrating a passion for justice, spirituality, beauty, the proper and humanizing exercise of power, and so on, then it will be apparent not only that they mean what they say, but that the God of whom they speak is indeed present, however mysteriously, and working in the world to accomplish his new creation.

What I have tried to do in this little book, then, is to ground this whole line of thought in John's gospel in particular. John's is the gospel of creation and new creation, of "witness" to Jesus and thence to the Father, of the Greeks coming to the feast and the victory over the dark powers. We have explored these themes in relation to both Jesus himself and the many people who came into contact with him during his public career, in some cases with vivid conversations and transformative impact. My hope and prayer as this book goes forward is that many who read it will themselves be led, perhaps through quiet meditation on John's gospel, not only to a deeper faith and hope for themselves, but to work on these vocations in their own communities. Justice, love, spirituality, beauty, freedom, truth, and power need not remain as elusive as they sometimes appear. By the power of the Spirit of Jesus the Messiah, crucified and risen from the dead, they can become genuine signposts, mended signals, missional marker posts. They will point all the more clearly, in the mercy of God, to the cross of Jesus and also to his resurrection as the start and the sign of the new creation. That "witness" is John's way of addressing one of the central tasks of the church: to show the wider world, in action and in speech, that the events concerning Jesus make sense of the world we know. They are not about escaping from creation. They are about its fulfillment.

These events, in fact, do with the world's puzzled questionings ("What is justice? Why doesn't it work?" and so on) exactly what

Jesus did with Nathanael, Nicodemus, the woman of Samaria, and many others, ending with Pontius Pilate himself. The story of Jesus, as John tells it, takes the questions very seriously, so seriously that he regularly digs down to the real question underneath in order to give the truest answer.

The story of Jesus thus offers a new framework for understanding the world—the framework of victory over corruption and death itself and the launching of the new creation. The old questions were the right ones to ask. They indicate a deep human sense that the world is not, after all, as it was meant to be. That intuition is correct. That is why the signposts appear broken. John tells us what the creator God has done, is doing, and will do, through his Son and his Spirit, to put things right. The signposts, duly straightened out, will then provide us with the template for our Spirit-led mission, sent into the world as the Father had sent the Son.

Scripture Index

Scripture Index